PURITAN DEVOTION

The Fernley-Hartley Lecture 1957
A Synopsis of which was delivered at
Derby Road Methodist Church, Lenton, Nottingham
on 16th July 1957

PURITAN DEVOTION

ITS PLACE IN THE DEVELOPMENT
OF CHRISTIAN PIETY

by

GORDON STEVENS WAKEFIELD
M.A., B.LITT.

LONDON : THE EPWORTH PRESS

THE EPWORTH PRESS
(FRANK H. CUMBERS)
25-35 City Road, London, E.C.1

MELBOURNE   CAPE TOWN
NEW YORK   TORONTO

SET IN MONOTYPE BASKERVILLE AND PRINTED IN
GREAT BRITAIN BY THE CAMELOT PRESS LTD
LONDON AND SOUTHAMPTON

TO

MY WIFE,
THE MEMORY OF MY PARENTS,
AND
MY TEACHERS AND FRIENDS,
ESPECIALLY
ROBERT NEWTON FLEW
AND
ERNEST GORDON RUPP

PREFACE

I AM deeply grateful to the Trustees for the honour they
have done me in inviting me to deliver the Fernley-Hartley
Lecture at the Methodist Conference of 1957. They have
given me the opportunity to publish a book on a subject which has
occupied such time as I have been able to devote to it for a number
of years, and which is of relevance to the pastoral ministry in the
midst of which the following pages have been written. This may
not excuse their many imperfections, but it may help to elucidate
their aims. I dare to hope that the book may make some contribution to various ends:

(1) As a Methodist, giving a Conference lecture, I have in mind
the fact that John Wesley knew and loved the great Puritans,
issued selections from their works in his *Christian Library*, and used
them as helps in his own teaching, as when he based a course of
sermons on Robert Bolton's *Directions for a Comfortable Walking
with God*. The theology of the Puritans formed part of what
Bernard Lord Manning once called 'the massive foundation of his
(Wesley's) instructed faith', and it is not presumptuous to suggest
that its study may be of help to his spiritual heirs even in these
days of Bultmann and the Dead Sea Scrolls. Some of us are
coming increasingly to value that Methodist tradition of which
Adam Clarke and Thomas Jackson are representatives, which
cherished the English Liturgy, and reconciled in a common in-
debtedness the Puritans and those whom posterity distinguishes
as the Anglican divines.

(2) I believe that the Wesleyan Fernley Lecture was first
instituted to be a guide to the ministers ordained at the Conference
of its delivery. The authors with whom we are concerned were
predominantly pastors, and therefore a study of them seems
peculiarly in keeping with the lectureship's foundation. Our
pastoral problems are doubtless more complex than those of the
Elizabethans and Stuarts, when Factory Chaplaincies were not
necessary, and Youth Work was not invented. Yet the fundamental questions which attack the Christian conscience do not
change with outward things. The examination of past methods,

though we can sometimes, and gladly correct them in the light of new knowledge, is better for us than a sole reliance on the latest text-book of psychology, or industrial mission pamphlet, or our own reminiscences.

(3) The republication of Puritan teaching may be of help to those in all communions who are 'seekers', and to whom the knowledge and love of God in Christ are beyond their chief joy. Some may not have suspected that Protestantism, much less Puritanism, could be the nurse of an intense and ardent piety.

(4) The great movement toward Christian Unity has taught us to respect and love each other's traditions. This book tries to discover the marks of a distinctively Puritan devotion. But it is offered as a modest effort toward ecumenical understanding, and to the greater glory of the Love which 'renders all distinctions void'.

A first essay in this field was accepted by the University of Oxford for the degree of Bachelor of Letters in 1954. That has been completely re-written and much amplified for the present purpose. Some of the material used appeared in four articles contributed to the *Preacher's Quarterly* in 1955.

I am indebted to a galaxy of scholars who at various times have fostered, encouraged, and criticized my efforts. Paramount is Dr R. Newton Flew, past Principal of Wesley House, Cambridge, who bore with me for three years in college, and suggested the Puritans as a subject of post-graduate study. He has most kindly read the first draft of this manuscript and made invaluable suggestions, but above all has given me, throughout the period of our friendship, the example of one who, in spite of his great distinction in all the Churches, has never lost the pastoral Heart. Then there are my Oxford supervisors: Dr Ernest A. Payne, now General Secretary of the Baptist Union, and Principal John Marsh of Mansfield College. Dr Marsh has read the manuscript, and has given me without stint the benefit of his scholarly judgement and generous friendship. The Warden of Keble College, the Reverend Eric S. Abbott, most kindly read the first draft. Professor Claude Jenkins, Dr Nathaniel Micklem, and Dr Geoffrey F. Nuttall have all given help when needed, though the present work does not in any sense bear their *imprimatur*. Finally, there is Professor Gordon Rupp, the brilliance of whose mind is only excelled by the generosity of his heart. As teacher, examiner, and friend he has been a constant inspiration. Needless to say none of the above is in any way responsible for my errors!

I must pay tribute to the many typists whose aid has willingly been given at various stages. As for my wife, she has had in some measure to live with the Puritans ever since our honeymoon. She has shown herself throughout deserving of the tribute which Richard Baxter paid to Margaret, and has 'heaped on me . . . many and great obligations to love and tenderness'.

GORDON S. WAKEFIELD

STOCKPORT
Advent 1956

CONTENTS

ABBREVIATIONS

MHB=Methodist Hymn Book (1933)
SJT=Scottish Journal of Theology

SELECT BIBLIOGRAPHY

PURITAN SOURCES

ADAMS, THOMAS (1612-53). Eloquent preacher, with a less utilitarian style than many Puritans. 'The prose Shakespeare of Puritan theologians' (Southey).
Workes (London, 1630).

AMBROSE, ISAAC (1591-1663). Lancashire Nonconformist of contemplative disposition.
Works (London, 1701).
Looking unto Jesus, a view of the Everlasting Gospel or the Soul's Eying of Jesus, as carrying on the great work of man's salvation from first to last (Glasgow, 1758).

AMES, WILLIAM (1576-1633). Disciple of Perkins. Inhibited by the Bishop of London, and retired to Holland. Casuist.
The Marrow of Sacred Divinity, drawne out of the Holy Scriptures, and the Interpreters thereof . . . translated out of the Latin (London, 1642).
Conscience with the Power and the Cases Thereof . . . translated out of the Latin (London, 1643).

BAXTER, RICHARD (1615-91). Eminent Pastor. A 'moderate episcopalian' and apostle of unity. Could not conform in 1662.
Reliquiae Baxterianae, ed. M. Sylvester (1696).
Autobiography, ed. J. M. Lloyd Thomas (1931).
Practical Works, ed. W. Orme (1830).
Poetical Fragments (13th edn, 1699).

BAYLY, LEWIS (?-1631). See Introduction.
The Practice of Piety (London, 1669).

BAYNES, PAUL (d. 1617). Perkins's successor at Great St Andrews, Cambridge. Thrust out of public ministry before he died.
Christian Letters (London, 1628).

BOLTON, ROBERT (1572-1631). Oxford Man. Converted after great struggle. Model of pastoral piety at Broughton, Northants.

Workes (London, 1641).

In the text *'Directions'* stands for *Directions for a Comfortable Walking with God.*

BROOKS, THOMAS (1608-80). Preacher with interest in the spiritual reformer Everard.

Works, ed. A. B. Grosart (1866).

BUNYAN, John (1628-88). *Works*, ed. G. Offor (1853).

CHARNOCK, STEPHEN (1628-80). Famous and prolific theologian, who spent some time in Ireland.

Works, ed. McCosh (1864).

DOD, JOHN (1550-1645). See Introduction.

The Ten Commandments (London, 1604).

A Plaine and Familiar Exposition on the Lord's Prayer (London, 1625).

DOWNAME, JOHN (d. 1652).

A Guide to Godliness, or a Treatise of a Christian Life (London, 1622).

The Christian's Warfare (London, 1609).

GOODWIN, JOHN (1593-1665). Arminian Vicar of St Stephen's, Coleman Street. 'A man by himself.' Controversialist of enlightened views, much misunderstood.

The Divine Authority of the Scriptures Asserted, or the Great Charter of the World's Blessedness Vindicated (1648).

Redemption Redeemed, An exposition of the 9th Chapter of the Epistle to the Romans (1653).

GOODWIN, THOMAS (1600-80). Sought refuge in Holland 1639. A moderate Calvinist in the Westminster Assembly. President of Magdalen College Oxford during the Commonwealth.

Works (London, 1866).

GOUGE, WILLIAM (1575-1653). Fellow of King's Cambridge, Minister of Blackfriars for forty-six years. One of the Feoffees for buying up advowsons, and as such prosecuted. Member of Westminster Assembly.

Workes (London, 1627).

A Guide to Goe to God, or an Explanation of the Perfect Patterne of Prayer, the Lord's Prayer (1626).

GREENHAM RICHARD (1535?-1594?). See Introduction.
Workes (London, 1601).

HOOKER, THOMAS (1586?-1647). Emigrated to New
England.
*The Application of Redemption by the effectual work of the Word and
Spirit of Christ, for the bringing home of lost sinners to God* (Books IX
and X, London 1656).

KEACH, BENJAMIN (1640-1704). See Chapter 2.
Tropologia, or a Key to Open Scripture Metaphors (London, 1681).

KING, BENJAMIN. Hertfordshire Minister.
The Marriage of the Lambe (London, 1640).

MANTON, THOMAS (1620-77). Oxford graduate and
London preacher. Member of Savoy Conference. Dissenter
after 1662.
How Ought we to Improve our Baptism (London, 1844).

MARSHAL, WALTER (1628-80). See Introduction.
The Gospel Mystery of Sanctification (London, 1692). (Referred
to as *Gospel Mystery*.)

OWEN, JOHN (1616-83).
Works, ed. W. H. Goold (London, 1851).

PERKINS, WILLIAM (1558-1602). See Introduction.
Workes (In one vol., London, 1605).
Workes (In three vols., London, 1617-26).

PRESTON, JOHN (1587-1628). See Introduction.
The Saint's Daily Exercise (1629).
The New Covenant (1630).
The Cuppe of Blessing (1633).
A Preparation to the Lord's Supper: Preached in Three Sermons (1638).
Grace to the Humble as Preparation to Receive the Sacrament (1639).
Mount Ebal or a Heavenly Treatise of Divine Love (1638).
A Heavenly Treatise of the Divine Love of Christ (1640).

ROUS, FRANCIS (1579-1659). See Chapter 6.
The Mysticall Marriage (1635).

RUTHERFORD, SAMUEL (1600-61). Pastor at Anwoth on
the Solway. Member of Westminster Assembly. Vehement
Controversialist. Passionate devotion, but anti-mystic.
Christ Dying and Drawing Sinners to Himselfe (1647).
Letters, ed. A. A. Bonar (1891).

SIBBES, RICHARD (1577-1635). Preacher at Gray's Inn, Master of Katherine Hall. Reputation of unsullied piety.
  The Spouse, Her Earnest Desire after Christ her Husband (1638).
  Works, ed. A. B. Grosart (1862).
SMITH, HENRY (1560-91). Oxford man, pupil of Greenham. Famous lecturer at St Clement Danes, 'but one metal below St Chrysostom himself'.
  Sermons (London, 1615).
  Works (Edinburgh, 1867).
STENNETT, JOSEPH (1663-1717). Baptist author of first published collection of eucharistic hymns.
  Hymns in Commemoration of the Sufferings of Our Blessed Saviour Jesus Christ, Composed for the Celebration of His Holy Supper. (*Works*, 1733 edn. Volume IV.)
VARIOUS.
  A Garden of Spirituall Flowers (1625 edn).
  The Marrow of Moderne Divinity (1902 edn).
VINES, RICHARD (1599-1655). Scholar and statesman employed in Parliamentary negotiations with Charles I.
  A Treatise of the Right Institution, Administration and Receiving of the Sacrament of the Lord's Supper delivered in XX Sermons at St Lawrence Jewry (1657).

STUDIES IN PURITANISM AND RELATED HISTORY

BARCLAY, ROBERT. *The Inner Life of the Religious Societies of the Commonwealth* (London, 1879).
BURGESS, W. H. *John Smith the Se-Baptist* (London, 1911).
DAKIN, A. *Calvinism* (London, 1940).
DAWLEY, P. M. *John Whitgift and the Reformation* (London, 1955).
DAVIES, HORTON. *The Worship of the English Puritans* (London, 1948). (Referred to as Horton Davies.)
DAVIS, A. P. *Isaac Watts* (London, 1948).
HALLER, WILLIAM. *The Rise of Puritanism* (New York, 1938).
  Liberty and Reformation in the Puritan Revolution (New York, 1955).
HUEHNS, GERTRUDE. *Antinomianism in English History* (London, 1952).
KNAPPEN, M. M. *Tudor Puritanism* (Chicago, 1939).

LEGG, J. WICKHAM. *English Church Life*, 1660-1833 (London, 1914).

McLACHLAN, H. J. *Socinianism in Seventeenth-century England* (Oxford, 1951).

MARTZ, L. L. *The Poety of Meditation* (London, 1954).

MAXWELL, W. D. *John Knox's Genevan Service Book, 1556* (Edinburgh, 1931).

MAYCOCK, A. L. *Nicholas Ferrar* (London, 1938).

MILLER, PERRY. *The New England Mind* (New York, 1939).

MILLER, PERRY, and JOHNSON, T. H. (eds). *The Puritans* (New York, 1938).

NUTTALL, G. F. *The Holy Spirit in Puritan Faith and Experience* (Oxford, 1947). (Referred to as Nuttall.)

OWST, G. R. *Literature and Pulpit in Medieval England* (Cambridge, 1933).

PAUL, ROBERTS. *The Lord Protector* (London, 1955).

PEEL, A., and CARSON, L. H. (eds). *Cartwrightiana* (London, 1951).

RUPP, E. G. *Studies in the Making of the English Protestant Tradition* (Cambridge, 1947).

Luther's Progress to the Diet of Worms, 1521 (London, 1951).

SIMPSON, ALAN. *Puritanism in Old and New England* (Chicago, 1955).

SMALLEY, BERYL. *The Study of the Bible in the Middle Ages* (2nd edn, Oxford, 1952).

SMYTH, CHARLES. *Cranmer and the English Reformation under Edward VI* (Cambridge, 1925).

The Art of Preaching (London, 1940).

Church and Parish (London, 1955).

TALON, HENRI. *John Bunyan, L'Homme et L'Oeuvre* (edn *Je Sers*, Paris; E.T., London, 1951).

TAWNEY, R. H. *Religion and the Rise of Capitalism* (Pelican edn, London, 1942).

TREVOR-ROPER, H. R. *Archbishop Laud, 1573-1675* (London, 1940).

WEBER, MAX. *The Protestant Ethic and the Spirit of Capitalism* (London, 1930; trans. Talcott Parsons).

WHITE, H. C. *English Devotional Literature, 1600-40* (Wisconsin, 1931).

WOODHOUSE, A. S. P. *Puritanism and Liberty* (London, 1938).

B

THEOLOGIA SPIRITUALIS

AQUINAS, THOMAS. *Summa Theologica* (E.T., Dominican Fathers, 1911-25).

BENOÎT, J. D. *Direction Spirituelle et Protestantisme: Etude Sur La Légitimité d'une Direction Protestante* (Paris, 1940). *Calvin, Directeur D'Ames* (Paris, 1944).

BONHOEFFER, D. *Ethics* (London, 1955).

BURNABY, J. *Amor Dei: A Study of St Augustine's Teaching on the Love of God as the Motive of the Christian Life* (Reprinted, London, 1947).

BREMOND, H. *Histoire Littéraire du Sentiment Religieux en France* (E.T., Vols. I-III, K. L. Montgomery, London, 1928).

CALVIN, J. *Institutes of the Christian Religion* (Trans. and ed. H. Beveridge, 2 vols., Reprinted, London, 1949).

CHADWICK, W. O. *John Cassian* (Cambridge, 1951).

COATS, R. H. *Types of English Piety* (London, 1912).

D'ARCY, M. C. *The Mind and Heart of Love* (London, 1944).

DAVIES, H. (S.J.). *Moral and Pastoral Theology* (London 1935).

DILLISTONE, F. W. *Christianity and Symbolism* (London, 1955).

DIX, GREGORY. *The Shape of the Liturgy* (London, 1945).

DODDRIDGE, P. *The Rise and Progress of Religion in the Soul* (1798 edn).

EVERARD, J. *The Gospel Treasury Opened, or the Holyest of all Unveiling* (ed. Rapha Harford, London, 1659).

FLEW, R. N. *The Idea of Perfection in Christian Theology* (Oxford, 1934).

FROST, BEDE. *The Art of Mental Prayer* (Reprinted London, 1950).

GEORGE, A. R. *Communion with God in the New Testament* (London, 1953).

GUEVARA, BISHOP. *The Mount of Caluerie*, compiled by the Rev. Father in God, Lord Anthonie de Guevara, Bishop of Modennedo, Preacher, Chronicler and Counsellor unto Charles the Fifth, Emperor (London, 1618).

HEILER, F. *Prayer* (London, 1932; E.T. of *Das Gebet*).

HOOKER, RICHARD. *Works* (1723 edn).

HÜGEL, F. von. *The Mystical Element in Religion* (London, 1908). *Essays and Addresses in the Philosophy of Religion*. 1st and 2nd Series (London, 1921, 1926).

INGE, W. R. *Christian Mysticism*, Bampton Lectures, 1899 (1948 edn).

JONES, R. M. *Spiritual Reformers in the Sixteenth and Seventeenth Centuries* (London, 1914).

KIRK, K. E. *The Vision of God*, Bampton Lectures, 1928 (London, 1931).

Some Principles of Moral Theology (London, 1920).

Beauty and Bands (London, 1955).

KNOX, R. A. *Enthusiasm* (Oxford, 1950).

LOYOLA, ST IGNATIUS OF. *Spiritual Exercises* (ed. W. H. Longridge, London, 1950).

McADOO, H. R. *The Structure of Caroline Moral Theology* (London, 1949).

MASCALL, E. L. *Christ, the Christian and the Church* (London, 1946).

Corpus Christi (London, 1953).

MERSCH, E. *The Whole Christ* (E.T., London, 1938).

MICKLEM, N. (ed.). *Christian Worship* (Oxford, 1936).

NYGREN, A. *Agape and Eros, The Study of the Christian Idea of Love* (E.T., A. G. Hebert and P. S. Watson; London, 1932-9).

PIERCE, C. A. *Conscience in the New Testament* (London, 1955).

POURRAT, P. *Christian Spirituality* (E.T., Mitchell and Jacques, 3 vols; London, 1922-7).

RATTENBURY, J. E. *The Eucharistic Hymns of John and Charles Wesley* (London, 1948).

SALES, ST FRANCIS OF. *Introduction to a Devout Life* (various edns).

SCOUGAL, H. *The Life of God in the Soul of Man* (5th edn, London, 1707).

SMYTH, CHARLES. *The Friendship of Christ* (London, 1945).

TAPPERT, T. G. (ed.). *Luther's Letters of Spiritual Counsel* (London, 1955).

TORRANCE, T. F. *Kingdom and Church* (Edinburgh, 1956).

WATSON, P. S. *Let God be God! The Theology of Martin Luther* (London, 1947).

WATTS, ISAAC. *Hymns and Spiritual Songs* (1731 edn).

Guide to Prayer (1722 edn).

WESLEY, JOHN. *A Christian Library: consisting of Extracts from and Abridgements of the Choicest Pieces of Practical Divinity which have been published in the English Tongue* (30 vol. edn. London, 1820).

WOOD, THOMAS. *English Casuistical Divinity during the Seventeenth Century* (London, 1952).

WOODHOUSE, H. F. *The Doctrine of the Church in Anglican Theology, 1547-1603* (London, 1954).

WHYTE, ALEXANDER. *The Spiritual Life; the Teaching of Thomas Goodwin as received and re-issued*, by Alexander Whyte (Edinburgh, 1917).

PAMPHLETS, ARTICLES, CHAPTERS

BEYREUTHER, ERICH. *Der Ursprung des Pietismus und die frage nach der Zeugenraft der Kirche* (*Evangelische Theologie*, September 1951).

BIGGS, W. W. *Preparation for Communion: A Puritan Manual* (*Congregational Quarterly*, January 1954).

DEMANT, V. A. *The Responsibility and Scope of Pastoral Theology Today* (Oxford, 1950).

FLEW, R. N. and DAVIES, R. E. (eds). *The Catholicity of Protestantism* (London, 1950).

GEORGE, A. R. *The Number of the Sacraments* (*Scottish Journal of Theology*, June 1951).

McLELLAND, J. C. *The Reformed Doctrine of Predestination according to Peter Martyr* (*Scottish Journal of Theology*, September 1955).

MILLER, PERRY. *Introduction to Jonathan Edwards's Images or Shadows of Divine Things* (Yale, 1949).

NUTTALL, G. F. *Richard Baxter and Philip Doddridge* (Oxford, 1951).

PAYNE, E. A. *The Anabaptists of the Sixteenth Century* (London, 1944).

PRESTIGE, G. L. *Eros: or Devotion to the Sacred Humanity* (*Fathers and Heretics*, Bampton Lectures, 1940; London, 1940).

SMYTH, CHARLES. *The Cambridge Puritans* (*Cambridge Review*, 1st February 1947).

WEST, W. MORRIS, S. *John Hooper and the Origins of Puritanism* (*Baptist Quarterly*, October 1954–April 1955).

WHALE, J. S. *Common Ground* (London, 1949).

PURITAN DEVOTION

The Old English Puritane was such an one that honoured God above all, and under God gave every one his due. His first care was to serve God, and therein he did not what was good in his own, but in God's sight, making the word of God the rule of his worship. He highly esteemed order in the House of God: but would not under colour of that submit to superstitious rites, which are superfluous and perish in their use. . . . He made conscience of all God's ordinances, though some he esteemed of more consequence. He was much in praier; with it he began and closed the day. In it he was exercised in his closet, family and publike assembly. He esteemed that manner of praier best, where by the gift of God, expressions were varied according to present wants and occasions; Yet he did not account set forms unlawful. Therefore in that circumstance of the Church he did not wholly reject the liturgy but the corruption of it. He esteemed reading of the word an ordinance of God both in private and publike; but he did not account reading to be preaching. . . . He accounted perspicuity the best grace of a preacher: And that method best which was most helpfull to understanding, affection and memory. . . . The Lord's day he esteemed a divine ordinance, and rest on it necessary so far as it induced to holinesse. He was very consciencious in the observance of that day as the Mart day of the Soul. . . . The Sacrament of Baptism he received in Infancy, which he looked back to in his age to answer his ingagements, and claim his priviledges. The Lord's Supper he accounted part of his soul's food: to which he laboured to keep an appetite. He esteemed it an ordinance of nearest communion with Christ, so requiring most exact preparation. . . . He accounted religion an engagement to duty, that the best Christians should be the best husbands, best wives, best parents, best children, best Masters, best servants, best Magistrates, best subjects, that the doctrine of God might be adorned not blasphemed. His family he endeavoured to make a Church, both in regard of persons and exercises, admitting none into it but such as feared God; and labouring that those that were born in it, might be born again to God. . . . He was a man of a tender heart, not only in regard of his own sin, but others' misery, not counting mercy arbitrary, but a necessary duty: wherein as he prayed for wisdom to direct him, so he studied for cheerfulnesse and a bounty to act. . . . In his habit he avoided costlinesse and vanity, neither exceeding his degree in civility nor declining what suited with Christianity, desiring in all things to expresse gravity. His whole life he accounted a warfare, wherein Christ was his captain, his arms, praiers and tears. The Crosse his Banner and his word *Vincit qui patitur.*

JOHN GEREE
The Character of an old English Puritane or Nonconformist
(1646)

CHAPTER ONE

INTRODUCTION

PURPOSE AND SOURCES

RECENT scholarship has rehabilitated the Puritans. The sumptuous volumes from across the Atlantic in which they are presented to the twentieth century should, by their massive learning and rare distinction of style, have banished certain misconceptions for ever from the minds of serious students.[1] No longer can the Puritan be intelligently portrayed as 'a gaunt, lank-haired kill-joy, wearing a black steeple-hat, and compounding for sins he was inclined to by damning those to which he had no mind'.[2] No longer can he be pilloried as the would-be *saboteur* of the Church of England, the fierce opponent of everything 'Anglican'.[3] The Puritan movement, like many throughout the Churches today, was no respecter of easily drawn confessional boundaries. Though the Restoration of 1660 seems to mark its political failure in England, its way of life has had an abiding influence, and the study of those who moulded the events of its tremendous years has been an inspiration in each subsequent century.

[1] See especially the works by William Haller, Perry Miller, M. M. Knappen, and A. S. P. Woodhouse, listed in the bibliography.

[2] Miller and Johnson, *The Puritans*, p. 2. The following stanza by Kenneth Hare, headed 'The Puritan' (Day Lewis and Strong, *New Anthology of Modern Verse*, 1920-40, edn 1944, p. 91), gives the popular idea:

> *The Puritan through life's sweet garden goes*
> *To pluck the thorn and cast away the rose*
> *And hopes to please by this peculiar whim*
> *The God who fashioned it and gave it him.*

Even G. G. Coulton in *The High Ancestry of Puritanism* (*Ten Medieval Studies*, 1915) regards Puritanism as the descendant of all that was most repulsive in medieval asceticism.

[3] H. R. McAdoo, *The Structure of Caroline Moral Theology* (London, 1949), begins by contrasting the Anglican approach to theology with others, including the Puritan, dismisses Perkins as a Puritan (p. 7), yet later, presses Bayly and Baxter into service (pp. 139-40, 148-9, 160, 167). P. E. More and F. L. Cross, *Anglicanism* (London, 1935), include passages from Baxter (pp. 84, 324, 413, 449, etc.). The name 'Anglican' seems first to have been used by F. D. Maurice and Charles Kingsley in the nineteenth century (see A. R. Vidler, *Witness to the Light* (New York, 1948), p. 202).

All this the writers from the New World demonstrate with ample
documentation. But their prime interest is social history rather
than the Christian religion, and sometimes the reader has cause to
suspect that the intensity of Puritan religious experience baffles
them, and they react to it with the urbane irony of cultured
sceptics at a revival meeting.[4] The modern Anglican and Roman
Catholic may understand Puritan devotion better than the
modern humanist. The purpose of this book is to describe and
evaluate Puritan ascetic theology in the hope that the study may
be profitable to the heirs of the Puritans' opponents, as well as to
their own numerous spiritual progeny.

There have been several recent studies in this field, most
notably Dr G. F. Nuttall's *The Holy Spirit in Puritan Faith and
Experience* (1946) and Dr Horton Davies's *The Worship of the
English Puritans* (1948). Dr Nuttall, however, is concerned with a
particular doctrine, and, naturally, most of his references come
from its climactic period, 1640-60. Dr Davies's volume deals with
the more public offices of Puritan piety. There seems room for a
book which will describe the wider aspects of Puritan devotion,
and to some extent avail itself of other sources than those used by
Dr Nuttall and Dr Davies. The following chapters will consider
the place of Scripture, Church, and Sacraments, in Puritan piety,
with a glance at the ordering of the household, and then go on to
discuss prayer and meditation, casuistry, and the goal of the
Christian life as the Puritans conceived it. We shall note some of
the sources of Puritan teaching and assess the Puritan contribution to 'the great Church'.

The selection of authors from an innumerable multitude has
been governed by the following considerations:

(1) Certain writers cannot be ignored because of their outstanding genius and universal fame. Such are Richard Baxter
(1615-91) and John Bunyan (1628-88). But it is important to
remember how much of the teaching of their predecessors and
contemporaries such men gather up.

---

[4] On the whole this is not true of Professor William Haller, but no Christian
theologian could be wholly at ease with the following passage from Professor Alan
Simpson's delightful *Puritanism in Old and New England* (Chicago, 1955): He quotes
Perkins's exposure of the error that 'If a man be no adulterer, no thief, nor murderer,
and does no man harm, he is a right honest man' and then comments: 'This last
seems an innocent enough sentiment until we recall that from Perkins's point of
view this man is simply a beautiful abomination as long as he remains unconverted'
(p. 8).

(2) The Cambridge Puritans of Elizabeth I's reign are particularly important, not only because they were the pioneers of Puritanism in the narrow sense, but because they began the Reformed study of pastoral theology and casuistry in England. In the next century, Jeremy Taylor acknowledged their books of cases of conscience.[5] Not all whose spiritual ministry was powerful in its generation have left behind writings of particular value, but there are important works by William Perkins (1558-1602), who was the greatest Puritan theologian of all; Richard Greenham (1535?-94?), a pastor and teacher of pastors, whose ministry at Dry Drayton is as attractive as that of George Herbert later at Bemerton; Henry Smith (c. 1560-91), an Oxford pupil of Greenham's, who was something of a Puritan counterpart to Lancelot Andrewes in the art of preaching;[6] Paul Baynes (d. 1617), who was Perkins's successor at Cambridge; and William Ames (1576-1633), who continued Perkins's work as a moral theologian.

(3) The divisions between Puritans have been interpreted in terms of French politics in the Third Republic, and references made to Puritans of the right, the centre, and the left.[7] By the time of the Civil Wars these differences fully emerged, and became politically irreconcilable. But even so, some of the extremists of this period considered themselves the heirs of the great Puritan pastors and spiritual guides. Hugh Peters, one of Cromwell's chaplains, who alone of his kind was considered too dangerous to live after the Restoration, bequeathed to his daughter *A Dying Father's Last Legacy to an Onely Child* (1660), in which he advised her to gather 'a little English Library' of Puritan authors— John Dod, Richard Sibbes, John Preston, William Gouge, Thomas Hooker, Thomas Goodwin, and Richard Baxter among them. Baxter and Peters would have disagreed on many things, but these authors are recommended in Baxter's own longer list of 'Affectionate, Practical, English writers'.[8] These are our men.

(4) It is Puritans of this kind whom John Wesley included in his *Christian Library*, and so it is this aspect of Puritanism which is of particular concern to Methodists. The *Library* has

[5] Jeremy Taylor, *Works* (1862 edn), IX.vi. I owe this reference to the Rev. H. Trevor Hughes, Principal of Westminster College, London.
[6] See Charles Smyth, in Rawlinson and Smyth, *The Genius of the Church of England* (London, 1947), p. 51, note 14.
[7] First by A. S. P. Woodhouse, *Puritanism and Liberty* (1938), Introduction, pp. 16 ff. Dr Nuttall uses the same terminology, op. cit.
[8] *Works*, V.587.

selections from Robert Bolton, John Preston, Richard Sibbes, Thomas Goodwin, Thomas Manton, William Dell, Isaac Ambrose, John Owen, Samuel Rutherford (the Scot), Richard Baxter, Samuel Charnock, Joseph Alleine, Richard Alleine, and John Howe. We have used the works of such of these men as seemed most relevant to our purpose. In addition it seemed profitable to examine the works of John Goodwin, who though not primarily a devotional and pastoral writer, was an Arminian, and has been regarded as the Wyclif of Methodism! Thomas Jackson wrote his life. In any case, John Goodwin brings some remarkable anticipations of modern critical method to the understanding of the Scriptures.

(5) We shall also draw upon some of the Puritan manuals of devotion. These are representative, and summarize the teaching of the Puritan leaders. Three in particular are valuable, published at different stages in the history of Puritanism. The earliest extant edition of *A Garden of Spirituall Flowers* is the fifth, dated 1609. The garden is, as the title-page has it, 'planted by Ri. Ro. (Richard Rogers), Will. Per. (William Perkins), Ri. Gree. (Richard Greenham), M. M. (unknown), Geo. Web. (George Webbe). Bishop Lewis Bayly's *The Practice of Piety*, was written about 1610, reached its 25th edition by 1630, its 59th in 1735, and was last reissued in 1842. It was translated into French in 1625, Welsh in 1630, German in 1629, Polish in 1647, and in 1665 at Cambridge, Massachusetts, it was turned into the tongue of the local Indians. This was one of the books which Bunyan's first wife brought him as a dowry.[9] Walter Marshal's *The Gospel Mystery of Sanctification* was not published until 1692, twelve years after its author's death. He was ejected at the Restoration, and became a Pastor at Gosport in Hampshire. His book is claimed to be the result of his own studies and spiritual struggles, and of the guidance he received from eminent Puritan Fathers. Alexander Whyte quotes two testimonials to the book's efficacy. One is from William Cowper, the eighteenth-century evangelical poet, who said of Marshal: 'I think him one of the best writers and the most spiritual expositor of Scripture I have ever read.'

[9] J. Bunyan, *Grace Abounding*, para. 15. Bayly died in 1631. He himself seems only to have preached piety, for in 1626 he was accused before the House of Commons on charges, 'which endorsed by Laud, and "palpably proved" in Parliament, included every kind of misdemeanour from licensing promiscuity in others to practising it himself' (H. R. Trevor-Roper, *Archibishop Laud* (1940), p. 188.

The other was uttered by an old Scotsman as he lay dying. He kissed his copy of Marshal's book and cried: 'O that Blessed Third Direction!'[10]

Occasionally we shall refer to other authors and treatises which illustrate particular themes of Puritan spirituality. We shall only go beyond the seventeenth century when a tendency of earlier Puritanism can be illustrated at its climax in Isaac Watts or Philip Doddridge, both of whom continue in a different age something of the 'passionate caring' and 'utter seriousness' of the earlier divines.[11]

Two other distinguished American scholars have not excluded the Puritans from scrutiny in surveys of devotional literature— Miss Helen C. White in her *English Devotional Literature 1600-40* (1931) and Professor Louis L. Martz in *The Poetry of Meditation* (1954)—but their aim is literary and their predominant interests are in a 'Catholic' direction. I do not think that they bring out the distinctive character of Puritan devotion as what follows attempts to do. Perhaps this is because they do not wholly understand Reformation Theology, and because it is easy for the eye to be dazzled by the splendours of contemporary French and Spanish spirituality, so brilliantly interpreted by Henri Bremond, Philippe Pourrat, and Allison Peers. It is tempting to see all that is edifying in Puritan piety as plagiarized from the Middle Ages or the Counter Reformation, and the rest as stunted by the 'horrible Decree'.[12] It is a popular notion that dies hard that the normative dogma of Reformed Christianity is that of Election, which is understood by expositors of other traditions as meaning essentially that only a few can be saved. The most recent research has established that the normative dogma is Union with Christ by Faith.[13] This is a clue that we shall follow in our study of the Puritans and it may lead us to distinguish a spirituality which, while not scorning the masters of the 'Catholic' way, begins from different and evangelical presuppositions.

---

[10] A. Whyte, *The Spiritual Life* (Edinburgh, 1917), pp. 66, 154.

[11] The phrases are used by G. F. Nuttall, *Richard Baxter and Philip Doddridge* (London, 1951), p. 2.

[12] It should be understood that this is not a correct translation of Calvin's *'decretum horrible'*, where the adjective should be rendered 'awful' in the sense of 'awe-inspiring'.

[13] cf. T. F. Torrance, *Kingdom and Church* (1956), pp. 100 ff; also J. C. McLelland 'The Reformed Doctrine of Predestination according to Peter Martyr', *Scottish Journal of Theology*, VIII.III.255 ff.

SOME LIVING GUIDES TO GODLINESS

It will be useful if we amplify in the case of six influential divines the brief biographical notes given elsewhere, in order that some at any rate of our authors may appear clothed in flesh and blood, and not buried in the dusty mildewed pages of their collected works.

First is William Perkins, whose ministry in Cambridge dominated the memories of Puritans for the half-century after his premature death in 1602. We are tempted to smile at Fuller's description of him pronouncing 'the word "damn" with such an emphasis as left a doleful echo in his auditors' ears a good while after', but we must not caricature a most influential preacher, theologian, and above all, casuist, 'author of the first sustained attempt in English to present the subject in an orderly and comprehensive manner'.[14] Tradition has it that Perkins's youth was debauched. But if so the drunkard was converted, and became the measure of Spirit-filled orthodoxy, not only in England but in Protestant Europe, into whose languages his works were turned for the conversion of worldlings and the confusion of Rome.[15] William Ames in the preface to his own *Conscience with the Power and Cases Thereof* recalls the time when he heard Perkins 'so preach in a great Assembly of Students, that he instructed them soundly in the truth, stirred them up effectually to seek after godlinesse, made them fit for the kingdom of God; and by his own example shewed them, what things they should chiefly intend that they might promote true Religion in the power of it unto God's glory, and others' salvation'.

Richard Greenham (1535?-1594?) was a Fellow of Pembroke College, Cambridge, and Rector from 1570 to 1590 of the village of Dry Drayton. He seems to have been a minister of kindly and gentle disposition, earnest and grave, austere in self-discipline and the keeping of Sabbaths, but tender with his flock, and as able to draw an illustration from the sights and sounds of his village cure as to plumb the depths of the subconscious mind. He was a true physician of the afflicted conscience, quick to discern Satan's stratagems, and very much of the type of Chaucer's 'poure persoun'.

[14] T. Wood, *English Casuistical Divinity* (1952), p. 34.
[15] Martin Schmidt, 'England *und der deutsche Pietismus*', *Evangelische Theologie*, September 1953, p. 205 ff, mentions Wolfgang Mayer (1577-1653) of Basel, who had studied in Cambridge and began to translate Perkins into German.

His panegyrist, Henry Holland, who is not guilty of minimizing his hero's virtues, records that Greenham was anxious to train younger men in the spiritual ministry, and 'communicate his experience with them. . . . Young men came to live with him at Dry Drayton, forming a kind of school, the members of which devoted themselves to the searching of the scripture and of one another's hearts'.[16] One of Greenham's pupils was Robert Browne, founder of an early group of separatists which took his name. It is tempting to speculate on whether, besides the surgery of souls, Browne learned at Dry Drayton those things which could divide the very joints and marrow of the State. But no teacher would wish to be held responsible for all his pupils' excesses, and in any case, Browne afterwards conformed.

Greenham's son-in-law was John Dod, sometime fellow of Jesus College, who, born in 1550, lived on into the Civil Wars and preached the funeral sermons of most of his contemporaries. To him was paid the greatest tribute that any preacher could crave: 'Poor simple people that never knew what religion meant when they had gone to hear him could not choose but talk of his sermon. It mightily affected poor creatures to hear the Mysteries of God . . . brought down to their own language and dialect.' More than a century after his death tracts were still being sold containing *The Worthy Sayings of Old Mr Dod, fit to be treasured up in the mind of every Christian.* These aphorisms are of the same artless simplicity as W. R. Maltby's famous answer to the question: 'Can Christians dance?'—'Some can and some can't!' Dod would tell friends who had come into money that though they had transferred from a boat to a ship they must remember that they were still on the sea. 'Brown bread and the Gospel is good fare.' 'Nothing can hurt us but sin, and that shall not hurt us if we can repent of it. And nothing can do us good, but the Love and Favour of God in Christ; and that we shall have if we seek it.' 'A man was never undone till in hell.' Two things he recommended to a married couple: Cares and Strifes. 'For the first let your cares be, which shall please God most; For your strifes, let them be which shall love God most and which shall love one another best; So will your cares and strifes be to purpose: So will all needless cares and strifes vanish.' John Dod's wit did not desert him in his nineties, and we can almost see the sparkle in his aged

---

[16] Quoted, W. Haller, *The Rise of Puritanism*, p. 28.

eyes the day he foiled some plundering Cavaliers, by removing a pair of sheets from the collected loot and sitting on them, while the soldiers searched the upper rooms of the house. Occasionally one seems to find the old man posing with a suggestion of smugness, though not like the typical Puritan of caricature, as when he refused to be shown Holmby House, preferring to sit still looking at a flower in his hand—'I see more of God in this flower than in all the beautiful edifices in the world'. But John Dod was the kind of pastor men wanted near them at the last.

John Preston (1587-1628) was one of the most brilliant of the Puritans who pleased King James I by maintaining the affirmative in a debate on 'whether brutes had reason or could make syllogisms?' His *tour de force* was the example of a dog, who, coming to the place where three ways meet, smells one way and then the other, and not finding the scent, runs down the third! It seems likely that Preston himself did a little sniffing out of the favours of the court. Political astuteness certainly went with prophetic preaching in his hectic career, and there was one brief period when he 'nearly caught the soul of Buckingham for God and the Great Seal for himself'.[17] He could not however oust Laud from the counsels of the malleable favourite, and had to be content with the Mastership of Emmanuel and a share in the moulding of the notorious William Prynne. Even if Preston's practical divinity involved him in the sordid intrigues of the day, he was no turncoat, and like some others, singed by baser flames, his heart was none the less on fire with the divine love, so that there is no wonder that Baxter regarded him as especially worth reading.[18]

Some of those whose works we shall use lived through the Civil Wars, the Commonwealth, and the Restoration. John Owen (1616-83) experienced ecclesiastical as well as political vicissitudes. While still within the Church of England he passed from Presbyterianism to Independency, and later knew outward changes of fortune to such an extent that he was Dean of Christ Church and Vice-Chancellor of Oxford University during the Commonwealth and a Dissenting minister after 1662. He was erudite, 'an Aristotle among Puritans', theologically orthodox and conservative. He engaged in an important controversy with Baxter on the subject of extempore prayer,[19] denying that liturgical

---

[17] H. R. Trevor-Roper, *Archbishop Laud* (1940), p. 160.
[18] Baxter, *Works*, XXII.4.   [19] There is an account of this in Nuttall, pp. 71 ff.

worship could be of the Holy Spirit. Owen's formal treatises do not warm the heart, but his real spiritual power is conveyed by his posthumously published sermons. And it is attractive to read of his gracious presence as well as of those sartorial vanities which make him very different from the imagined Puritan. 'As Vice-Chancellor of Oxford, if Wood is to be trusted, he went cloakless in order to show off his figure, powdered his hair, and wore large tassels on his bandstrings, pointed ribbons at his knees, Spanish leather boots with large lawn tops, and his hat mostly cock'd.'[20]

And so with the angle of John Owen's hat in our minds to keep us from thinking of the Puritans as altogether indifferent to the trivialities of the world, we will turn to the serious business of their lives, and ours.

[20] W. Haller, *Liberty and Reformation*, p. 337.

Christian saw the picture of a very grave person hang up against the wall; and this was the fashion of it: it had eyes lifted up to heaven, the best of books in its hand, the law of truth was upon its lips, the world was behind its back; it stood as if it pleaded with men, and a crown of gold did hang over its head.

JOHN BUNYAN

The history of the Israelites is our history; it is the history of the Church Universal.

CHRISTOPHER WORDSWORTH

CHAPTER TWO

THE SCRIPTURES AND PURITAN DEVOTION

THE PROTESTANT historian of Christian spirituality is liable to be embarrassed when he returns to the New Testament. Not that there is much neglect of Scripture among professed Christian ascetics; some of the earliest slept with the Bible under their pillows.[1] But the atmosphere of the New Testament is very different from that of the later piety of both East and West, which tends to represent the Christian life as an arduous ascent to perfection. The New Testament writers, and for that matter Hermas and Irenaeus as well, 'could not conceive the Christian life in terms of progress toward a goal, because they believed that the goal had already through God's acts been reached. The kingdom had come; the eschatological event, though its consummation was in the future, was also a present fact. The Christian had died to sin; he could be described as righteous, saintly, perfect.'[2] To use the terminology of Dr Nygren, the religion of the Christian ages tends to be *Eros*—or *Caritas*—religion, preoccupied with the upward striving of the soul; that of the New Testament is *Agape* religion, dominated by the descent of God's free grace. The design which St John of the Cross, the great Spanish mystic of the sixteenth century, intended for the frontispiece of his books shows a mountain, on the summit of which is perfect union with God. At the foot, three roads are revealed to the soul, but only one of them, the road of complete renunciation, leads to the summit. St John calls the mountain Carmel, but the reader of the New Testament may wonder whether it might not be the Sinai of bondage from which Christ sets us free.

The question at once arises whether there is any room for an ascetic system in the religion of those whose ultimate authority is Holy Scripture. The Catholic is not so troubled by this problem, because he reads the New Testament only under the Church's direction, and accords a place equally authoritative and inspired

---

[1] See P. Pourrat, *Christian Spirituality*, III.6.
[2] W. O. Chadwick, *John Cassian*, pp. 77-8.

to tradition. But the Protestant may be tempted to dismiss the whole development of *theologia spiritualis* as invalid. For example, the late Pierre Maury wrote in 1939, contrasting true and false ministries, that they were 'on the one hand a testimony given to what God has done for man, on the other a schoolmastering, a moulding of moral and religious personalities; on the one hand the preaching of the word of grace, plainly from Scripture, . . . on the other practical advice, pious exhortation, asceticism, and mysticism, which avail themselves of Jesus Christ, but do not serve him'.[3]

The Puritans regarded Scripture as the supreme and final authority. Like a wind from heaven the Bible seemed able to sweep away the corruptions and accretions of the unreformed Church. Here was the word of God, condemning the traditions of men and declaring His whole counsel. To the question how do we know that the Bible is the Word of God unless the Church vouch for it, the Puritans replied with Calvin's doctrines of the testimony of the Spirit and the self-evidencing power of Scripture. Richard Sibbes has a preacher's illustration: A carrier may show us letters which, he tells us, are from a certain friend. Thus speaks the Church. But it is when we open the letters and see the hand and seal that we are sure. So, when we read the Bible, the Spirit Himself convinces us that it is from God.[4] John Owen, writing *Of the Divine Original, Authority, Self-Evidencing Light, and Power of the Scriptures*, declares that 'God, speaking *in* the penmen of the Scripture (Hebrews 1[1]), his voice to them was accompanied with its own evidence which gave assurance unto them; and God speaking *by* them, or their writings unto us, his word is accompanied with its own evidence, and gives assurance unto us'. Owen seeks to prove

that the Scriptures of the Old and New Testament do abundantly and uncontrollably manifest themselves to be the Word of the living God; so that, merely on account of their own proposal of themselves unto us, in the name and majesty of God, as such—without the contribution of help or assistance from tradition, church, or anything else without themselves,—we are obliged upon the penalty of eternal damnation

---

[3] P. Maury, *Foi et Vie*. Quoted by J. D. Benoît, *Direction Spirituelle et Protestantisme* (Paris, 1940), p. 21. (My translation.)

[4] R. Sibbes, *Works*, II.494; cf. Calvin *Institutes*, I.vii.4: 'For as God alone can properly bear witness to his own words, so these words will not obtain full credit in the hearts of men, until they are sealed by the inward testimony of the Spirit.'

(as are all to whom by any means they come, or are brought) to receive them with that subjection of soul which is due to the word of God.[5]

The Puritans had high regard for the Fathers, but would never urge their authority 'for necessity of proof or as Divine Law'.[6] True, some are more 'liberal' than Owen, and Richard Baxter anticipates the conclusions of more recent scholarship when he says 'Something must be taken upon trust from men' and 'Tradition is not so useless to the world or to the Church as some would have it'.[7] But Puritanism starts from the absolute sufficiency and supreme authority of Scripture. One of the earlier protagonists, William Bradshaw, thus describes the position he regards as characteristic of the Puritans: 'IMPRIMIS they houlde and maintaine that the word of God contained in the writings of the Prophets and Apostles, is of absolute perfection, given by Christ, the Head of the Churche, to be unto the same the sole Canon and rule of all matters of religion and of the worship and service of God whatsoever.'[8]

In spite of this, the Puritans did not draw M. Maury's deduction. For one thing, the conditions of historical existence itself seldom allow the past to be without influence, albeit unconscious, or curb entirely the cross-fertilization of ideas. And the very legalism of the Puritan attitude to Scripture, in which they out-Calvined Calvin,[9] made them try to derive from it an ascetic system of their own. A twentieth-century theologian, with his acute historical sense, will inevitably select from Scripture the leading ideas and unifying doctrines, and will discard or relegate

[5] J. Owen, *Works*, XVI.307; cf. Calvin, *Inst.*, I.7.2: 'Scripture bears upon the face of it as clear evidence of its truth, as white and black do of their colour, sweet and bitter of their taste.'

[6] cf. R. Bolton, *Foure Last Things*, p. 147. Henry Smith claims that the Fathers themselves teach the absolute sufficiency of the Scriptures (*Works*, II.430 ff). The attitude of the 'Anglican' Divines to the Fathers was not dissimilar—see H. F. Woodhouse, *The Doctrine of the Church in Anglican Theology, 1547-1603*, pp. 22-3.

[7] Baxter, *Works*, XXII.294-5; cf. Vincent Taylor, *Forgiveness and Reconciliation* (1946), p. xix: 'The New Testament writings have decisively shaped the life of the Church, but no less certainly has the Church influenced the formation, canon and text of the New Testament, and in some respects of the revelation contained therein.'

[8] W. Bradshaw (d.1618?), *English Puritanisme* (1605), p. 1. Bradshaw was an interesting person, whose chief concern was Church government. See *Dictionary of National Biography*.

[9] For Calvin's 'principle of accommodation' and the place of the Scriptures in his thinking, see E. Doumergue, *Jean Calvin*, II.499-502, IV.54-82; also A. Dakin, *Calvinism*, pp. 185 ff. N.B. The Puritans were 'legalists', not 'fundamentalists'; cf. Charles Smyth, *Church and Parish*, pp. 156 ff.

—sometimes dangerously—those passages which do not harmonize. Not that this procedure is wholly modern; Luther, as is well known, criticized elements in the Book of Esther, the Epistle of James, and the Revelation. But the Puritan, seeking a divine law to restrain the anarchy alike of the Church, the nation, and the human heart, could ignore no precept of the New Testament or the Old. And therefore, being less concerned with the synoptic view of Scripture than with the need to treat each precept as positive divine law, the Puritan had plenty of biblical justification for his asceticism. There are commands to renunciation in the Gospels, and encouragements to athletic training and holy war in the Epistles. Christ fasted in the wilderness, and called Himself the Way. And the Puritan did not regard the Old Testament as less binding than the New, because, like Calvin and to some extent the New Testament writers themselves, he believed that it revealed the same God and taught the things of Christ. Thus the nomadic wanderings of the Patriarchs and the wilderness journeyings of Israel represent the Christian pilgrims' progress toward their heavenly goal, and the fightings, and temptation by the way.

The Puritan's approach to Scripture, and his view of authority, made him use it as the basis of an ascetic theology. And if the words of Scripture demanded this, so did its silences. The Puritans would hesitate to deny the absolute sufficiency of Scripture, and we find Thomas Brooks declaring, somewhat, smugly, 'Where the Scripture is silent, there I love to be silent, and where the Scripture hath no tongue there I have no ears';[10] but in practice the pastor must resolve questions on which there is no direct guidance in the Bible, if only because neither the state of the world nor of the Church in the world is precisely what it was long ago. Thus an ascetic system was essential, and the conclusions of Scripture itself seemed to be those stated by William Gouge: 'God's assistance and man's endeavour concurre together; they may not be severed.'[11]

PRIVATE READING

Granted this, nothing was more important in the practice of Puritan piety than the reading of the Scriptures. Before the

[10] *Works*, IV.274.   [11] *Workes*, I.15.

Reformation, 'Richard Rolle's glossed English Psalter was the only book of the Bible that the laity might use without licence. Some gospel harmonies were licensed as safer reading for the laity than vernacular gospels'.[12] In the thirteenth century, there was a change in the technique of Christian devotion even for clergy and religious, and the emphasis came to be laid more on the hearing of Mass than the reading of the Bible, which need not be pursued once sufficient material had been gleaned from it for meditation.[13] This may well be reflected even so late as St Francis of Sales's *Introduction to a Devout Life*, published in 1609. The Bishop writes with his Bible in his hand; each meditation has a scriptural basis. But when we reach the section on hearing and reading the Word of God, though it includes a comment on listening to sermons which would have delighted a Puritan, we find merely a list of devotional books and nothing at all about the direct reading of the Bible.[14] For the Puritan, living at a time when the vernacular Bible was still a 'new thing' and bought by martyrs' blood, nothing could dispense with private reading. The doctrine of the testimony of the Holy Spirit meant that all could receive illumination, for this is no 'private whisper' but a 'public testimony'.[15] The translation which the Puritans used, and did not altogether discard even after the appearance of the Authorized Version in 1611, was the Geneva Bible, the work of Marian Exiles, first published as a whole in 1560. This Bible introduced the numbering of the verses, and included some 'most profitable annotations' clearly derived from the city of its origin. Both Greenham and Bayly expect the Bible to be read three times a

[12] Nuttall, p. 21, n.4.

[13] B. Smalley, *Bible in Middle Ages*, pp. 282 ff.

[14] 'Remember that our Lord gathers up the words we speak to Him in our prayers, according as we gather up those He speaks to us by preaching', Francis of Sales, op. cit., p. 90; cf. R. Greenham, *Workes*, p. 333: 'If we doe heare the Lorde, he will heare us.' A *Catholic Commentary on Holy Scripture* (Nelson, 1953), p. 11, declares: '. . . there is no universal precept . . . that all the faithful . . . should personally read the Bible.' Numberless Catholics lead good lives without any reading. 'They nourish their minds with the substance of the Bible through the Liturgy of the Mass, through the mysteries of the Rosary, through the prayers which they know by heart, and through the sermons which they hear.' On the other hand in the encyclical *Afflante Spiritu* (1943) Pope Pius XII is very strong on Bible study. The Bishops are to encourage Christian families in the habit of reading the Scriptures devoutly, every day (quoted R. N. Flew, ed., *The Nature of the Church* (1952), pp. 27-8).

[15] J. Owen, *Works*, XVI.328. Baxter's father apparently was converted 'by the bare reading of the Scriptures in private, without either Preaching or Godly Company, or any other Books but the Bible' (*Reliquiae Baxterianae*, I.1).

day, 'a chapter at a time'.[16] Thus, says Bayly, granted that 'so many Psalmes instead of a Chapter as our Church Liturgie appoints for Morning or Evening Prayer' are read, the whole Bible can be gone through in a year, 'except six chapters, which thou mayest add to the task of the last day of the year'.[17]

THE LETTER AND THE SPIRIT

The Puritans were not unaware of the difficulties of scriptural interpretation. Medieval exegesis had many different schemes to which the 'four senses' were basic. A famous example is Cassian's exposition of Jerusalem. According to the historical sense, Jerusalem is the city of the Jews; allegorically it is the Church of Christ; anagogically, that is with reference to the life of the world to come, it is the Heavenly City; tropologically or morally, it is the soul of man. The tendency during the Middle Ages, which of course reached its extremes in popular devotion and preaching, was to despise the historical sense as of 'the dead and killing letter', and to seek both edification and truth in allegory.[18] From this the Puritans, like the Reformers, broke free. They recognized that there are figures and allegories in Scripture itself, and in 1681, Benjamin Keach, minister of a Particular Baptist Church in London, and composer of eucharistic hymns, issued a redaction in three books of Salomon Glassius's *Philologia Sacra* (Jena, 1623-36) under the title *Tropologia: A Key to Open Scripture Metaphors and Types*. But the purpose of this was to analyse and resolve the existing allegories of the Bible, to penetrate the symbols and apprehend the saving word of faith— not to allegorize the literal meaning.

John Owen is especially jealous for the letter of the Scripture. The publication of Brian Walton's *Biblia Polyglotta* in 1653

---

[16] The modern division into chapters is usually credited to Stephen Langton (d. 1228)—see B. Smalley, *Bible in Middle Ages*, pp. 222 ff. For an account of the Geneva Bible and its significance in the evolution of the modern Bible, see *Ancient and English Versions of the Bible* (ed. H. W. Robinson, Oxford, 1940), pp. 181 ff, also *The Bible Today Considered by Christian Scholars* (London, 1955), pp. 132 ff.

[17] *The Practice of Piety*, pp. 114-15. Isaac Ambrose, *Works* (1701 edn), pp. 199 ff, has detailed instructions for reading and analyses of all the Bible books; cf. *A Plaine and Perfect Method for the easie understanding of the whole Bible: Containing Seven Observations, Dialogue-wise, betweene the Parishioner and the Pastor* (London, 1617).

[18] Cassian, *Collationes*, XIV.8, mentioned by B. Smalley, *Bible in Middle Ages*, p. 28; cf. Dante's explanation of the meaning of the Divine Comedy in a letter to his patron, quoted in D. L. Sayers's edn, I.14-5; cf. also G. R. Owst, *Literature and Pulpit*, pp. 57 ff, 114-15, Chapter 8.

compelled him to add a lengthy dissertation to his treatise on the
Divine Original of Scripture, because the display of variant readings
might seem to cast doubts upon the reliability of the sacred text,
and on whether we can claim to have anything like the un-
corrupted *ipsissima verba* of the inspired authors. Owen is bound
to acknowledge some alternative readings, but he sets out to
prove that these are in comparatively unimportant places, and
have been magnified by those who would seek to make Church
tradition the arbiter. He devotes many pages to establishing that
the Hebrew points are coeval with the letters, and were completed
by the scribe Ezra, 'guided therein by the infallible spirit of God'![19]
Elsewhere, he asserts that the saying in St Matthew's Gospel
about no jot or tittle passing away from the law is a divine
promise to protect the least letter, vowel or point of the sacred
writings![20] Nevertheless it is the Spirit and not the bare letter
which illumines. He alone imparts to the word 'virtue, power,
efficacy, majesty, and authority'.[21]

Earlier, William Gouge distinguishes between the letter and the
Word in the sense of the divine Message. He supports this by
noting discrepancies between our Old Testament version and the
New Testament quotations from the prophets. 'The letter of
Scripture may be alledged and yet the Word of God missed, as by
all heretiques. And a man may swerve from the letter and yet
alleadge the true word of God, as the Evangelists and the Apostles
did many times.'[22]

This embryonic criticism is carried a stage farther by Baxter,
who admits certain distinctions within Scripture between, for
instance, doctrine and the words which express it, the substantial
part of Scripture doctrine and the circumstantial, the direct sense
and the implied, the main scope 'and particular words and
phrases'.[23] Baxter will allow saving faith to several classes of
people who do not accept the infallibility of every part of Scripture
or who doubt whether the author's 'pens were as perfectly guided

---

[19] Owen, *Works*, XVI.371. The points were actually invented and inserted by the
Massoretes later than A.D. 500, but it is only fair to add that this fact was not determined in Owen's time.

[20] ibid., IV.213, 232.

[21] ibid., XVI.328; cf. R. Sibbes: 'As the spirits in the arteries quicken the blood in
the veins, so the Spirit of God goes along with the word and makes it work.' 'The
word is nothing without the Spirit; it is animated and quickened by the Spirit'
(*Works*, VII.193, 199).

[22] W. Gouge, *Workes*, I.154.

[23] *Works*, XXII.258 ff.

as their minds', even though he feels that such people are casting away a great support of faith.[24] He has, in a footnote, a most interesting exegesis of 2 Peter 1[20]: 'No prophecy of Scripture is of private interpretation.'[25] John Owen, following Calvin and Grotius, refers this Greek phrase to the way in which the prophets received their inspiration, not by rational understanding, nor by 'fancied enthusiasm', but by the will of God.[26] Baxter, on the other hand, considers that the words concern our interpretation of prophecy, but they do not seek to prohibit private individuals from interpreting Scripture; they assert that the prophets in their oracles do not speak of themselves, privately, but of Christ the 'public Person', representative of the human race. Modern renderings and comments endorse neither Baxter nor Calvin-Owen. The words mean simply that Scripture must not be interpreted by private caprice. But Baxter's exegesis is remarkable in its sensitiveness to the Scriptural conception of corporate personality, which is so much regarded by twentieth-century scholars.

John Goodwin is the frankest of all, and is the interpreter who comes nearest to what we understand by historical method.[27] 'The true and proper foundation of the Christian religion', he writes, 'is not inke and paper, nor any book or books, not any writing/or writings whatever, whether translations or originals; but that substance of matter, those gracious counsells of God concerning the salvation of the world by Jesus Christ, which indeed are represented and declared both in Translations and Originalls, but are essentially distinct from both and no waies for their natures and being depending on either of them.'[28] In a human contract, the writing is not the bargain; it only declares its terms and tenor. No book or writing in the world can be either in whole or in part the Word or Will of God. John Goodwin can even say that Bible reading is not necessary to faith and salvation, so anxious is he to deliver men from the tyranny of the letter.

A similar liberation is sought by a mysterious and fascinating

---

[24] *Works*, XXII.264-5.   [25] ibid., p. 294, note *n*.   [26] Owen, *Works*, XVI.303-4.
[27] e.g. his rules for the interpretation of Scripture at the end of his exposition of Romans 9 (1653). The historical method is not correctly described as 'modern' much less 'modernist'. It was applied by Theodore of Mopsuestia (d. 428) and the School of Antioch, but lost sight of, owing to certain condemnations for heresy, and the fact that the allegorical method of Alexandria 'satisfied a paramount emotional need and corresponded to a world outlook' (B. Smalley, op. cit., pp. 14 ff.)
[28] J. Goodwin, *The Divine Authority of the Scriptures*, p. 17.

personality who belongs in part to the spiritual underworld of the seventeenth century. This is John Everard, whose works were approved by Thomas Brooks, and whom William Haller counts as a Puritan, but who is perhaps better classed as a Spiritual Reformer.[29] Everard is constantly contrasting 'the dead and killing letter' with the Holy and life-giving Spirit. At times he reveals a violent anti-historicism and could be almost charged with denying that the things recorded in Scripture were actually done. He contends that we need 'a dayly doing all the Scriptures over again'. All the events of Christ's life on earth must have their counterpart within us, from the miraculous conception to the Cross. Apocalyptic describes spiritual rebirth.[30] Not that Everard would destroy the letter. It is the vehicle of the Spirit, and once we have that Divine Seal, we can no more throw away the letter than a man can kill the wife he loves. But these 'literal black letters' cannot 'possibly contain the Mighty, Eternal Majesty of the Word of God', which is Christ.[31]

This is not the authentic attitude of the Puritans. For them the Bible is a revelation given through things which happened in history, and which it exactly records. But the knowledge of such events is not enough. We must have a faith which sees *in history* the saving purpose of God. Thomas Goodwin writes of the death of Jesus, conspired not merely by the Jews and Pilate as a literal, history-faith would suggest, but by 'God his Father complotting with' Christ Himself and aiming at a higher end than did Christ's enemies.[32] The inner meaning of the Passion is not simply that our sins must be crucified, but that God justifies the ungodly and that Christ ever lives to apply this justification to our hearts. But we can see from these examples that the open Bible meant a diversity of interpretations, and that the Puritans were not to be wholly free from those difficulties and confusions of private judgement which Catholics so much dread.

THE RESTRAINT OF ERROR

The Puritans attempted to apply several correctives. One was the principle referred to earlier, and summarized in a famous phrase

---

[29] cf. Rufus M. Jones, *Spiritual Reformers*, pp. 239 ff.
[30] J. Everard, *Gospel Treasury* (1659 edn), pp. 75, 99.
[31] ibid., pp. 356 ff.
[32] *Works*, IV.19 ff.

of Luther's: 'Christ is the Lord of the Scriptures.'[33] Greenham recognizes that left to ourselves we can seek for the wrong things in Holy Writ, even as James and John asked for the favoured places in glory or the disciples said: 'Lord wilt thou at this time restore again the Kingdom to Israel?' Some things are not revealed; others are not profitable, such as burrowing among genealogies or talk of reforming the Church when we ourselves are unreformed. Faith in Christ must be the preliminary to reading. He is 'the Lion of the Tribe of Juda to whom it is given to open the Booke of God'.[34] So Sibbes declares: 'Christ is the spirit of the Scriptures, of all truths, of all ordinances.'[35] This for him reconciles the seeming contradictions of the Bible. How can the Law for instance be both dead as Paul asserts (2 Cor 3) and perfect according to the Psalmist (Psalm 19[7])? It is dead, even as the Gospel is a savour of death (2 Cor 2[15]) when unaccompanied by the Spirit; but once Christ was come, the Spirit worked no longer with the Law but with the Gospel.

The Geneva Bible has this marginal comment on Jacob's dream: 'Christ is the ladder whereby God and man are joined together, by whom the angels minister unto us; all graces by him are joined to us, and we by him ascend into heaven'; and Bunyan similarly writes: 'Christ is Jacob's ladder that reacheth up to heaven.'[36] A comparison with the very different use of Jacob's ladder by St Francis of Sales in his *Introduction* illustrates the important distinction between typology and allegory. St Francis sees the two sides of the ladder as prayer and the sacraments while the rungs are the progressive degrees of charity. This is allegorical exegesis. It belongs ultimately to the world of the imagination; it need not be Christological; it derives from Platonism. The Puritan's typology, on the other hand, which is in the tradition of Origen, Jerome, Erasmus, and Zwingli, is an attempt to see historic parallels between the Old Testament and the New. By looking into the events of the Hebrew Scriptures it gazes into the Face of Jesus Christ.

Admittedly the result is not always edifying. Some words of F. W. Robertson are a strident but not wholly unnecessary warning. 'There is nothing more miserable as specimens of perverted ingenuity than the attempts of certain commentators

---

[33] *Gal. Comm.* (E.T.), 179 (3[10]).   [34] R. Greenham, *Workes*, 204-5.
[35] *Works*, IV.210.   [36] *Works*, I.103.

and preachers to find remote and recondite and intended allusions to Christ everywhere [in the Bible]. . . . This perverted mode of comment is not merely harmless, idle, useless; it is positively dangerous. This is to make the Holy Spirit speak riddles and conundrums and the interpretation of Scripture but clever riddle-guessing.'[37] It is sometimes best to recognize that certain passages are sub-Christian and abandon all attempts to treat them as other than evidence of a spirit which cannot withstand the Cross. Bayly and Ames, for instance, like some present-day exegetes, try very hard to retain, with Christian meaning, the imprecatory Psalms. Bayly exhorts his readers to deal violently with their sins, and 'dash Babylon's children while they are yet young against the stones'.[38] Ames believes that we should use such passages to understand the terrible judgements of God against the impenitent, and His retributive justice, which in the end reverses the roles of the prosperous wicked and the afflicted godly. They are prayers to hasten the Divine vengeance against the enemies of the Church; to quote the title of a book by Father Benson of Cowley, they are *The War Songs of the Prince of Peace*.[39] Such interpretations are to be preferred to the mangling of the Psalter for the selection of edifying passages. Nor can the spiritual truths which they wrest from the verses be denied. The Bible is not merely improving literature, and the Lamb of God is a Lion in the Fight. The danger is that here typology will conceal what is incompatible with the ethics of the Gospel, and give a mandate to ruthlessness against the opponents of the Cross.

Secondly, the Puritans insisted that passages of Scripture should not be wrested from their context. 'The right context of Scripture is half the interpretation,' says Thomas Goodwin.[40] His namesake, John, in his Rules of interpretation, shows an amazing discernment of the Scriptural writers' habit of mind, and anticipation of the axioms of later scholarship. John Goodwin is not the tersest of writers and his rules are hardly aphorisms, so that direct quotation is not always illuminating; but as a sample of his insight, we may mention his statements that, in Scripture,

---

[37] F. W. Robertson, cited F. W. Farrar, *History of Interpretation* (1886), p. 334, n.1.
[38] Psalm 137⁹.
[39] W. Ames, *Conscience and the Cases Thereof*, IV.44. For a similar modern interpretation, cf. L. Bouyer, *The Paschal Mystery* (London, 1951), pp. 7 ff. R. M. Benson's book was published in 1901.
[40] *Works*, V.349; cf. W. Gouge, *Workes*, I.154.

sonship often refers to spiritual likeness, that secondary causes are sometimes ignored, and that individuals sometimes represent communities. He also has an acute understanding of syntax.

Thirdly, the Puritans believed that reading should be accompanied by prayer and meditation.[41] All that is read in Scripture must be applied, either to confirm faith or increase repentance, as though each passage were addressed particularly to the reader, and the words were spoken by God standing at his side. Richard Greenham lists eight properties for a faithful reading and hearing: '(1) Diligence, (2) Wisedome, (3) Preparation, (4) Meditation, (5) Conference, (6) Faith, (7) Practice, (8) Prayer'[42]—an interesting list, not least in its order, but there is no doubt that Greenham would regard Conference as among the more important safeguards. This means the fellowship of the Church, but 'This rule must be kept that conference with our equals must be of those things which we heard of our Ministers, as it must be kept also in meditation, which is a conference with ourselves. We must for a time like babes hang at the mouthes of the Ministers, because we cannot runne before we goe: nay we cannot goe without a leader.'[43] William Gouge is sure that no true interpretation of Scripture is possible without some knowledge of the original tongues,[44] and who has this but the minister who is trained for exposition? Thomas Goodwin, grieved by the numerous souls in distress through Scripture misunderstood and misapplied, bids them 'goe to some spiritual lawyer skilled in soul-work'.[45] We may notice the parallel with the old Monastic Collationes, the daily conferences at which the Abbot preached and the monks were allowed to ask questions suggested by their reading, and with the Zurich 'prophesyings' of Zwingli and Bullinger.

These safeguards did not secure unanimity among interpreters, nor restrain 'enthusiasts', nor bring peace to the labouring consciences of individuals. The first aim is neither legitimate nor desirable, and it was one of the weaknesses of the seventeenth century that its leaders, with rare exceptions, failed to see this. The truth of God's Holy Word, as John Robinson's famous words imply, is greater than our grasp of it, and, provided there is agreement on some few fundamentals such as the peculiar authority of Scripture, a diversity of interpretations held in

[41] Bayly, *The Practice of Piety*, p. 114.   [42] *Workes*, p. 203.
[43] ibid., 205.   [44] *Workes*, I.154.   [45] *Works*, III.319.

charity and love of truth adds only to the richness of Christ's Church.[46] Moreover it has never proved possible in Church history to prevent private interpretation or curb 'lay' movements, whether prophetic or disastrous. As for the struggles of individuals wrestling with the Word, the classic case is that of John Bunyan. He was not without 'Conference' in the Church at Bedford and with its pastor, and there is little reason to think, with all deference to Henri Talon's sensitive study, that Catholicism would have 'chased winter from his soul' any more than it did from Luther's.[47] Neither would a greater sense of history or of context in reading Scripture have helped him, for he read as much damnation from the New Testament as from the Old, and as much comfort from the Old Testament, interpreted by Christ, as from the New. The fact is, as the Puritans recognized equally with traditional Catholic piety, there is a period of lone darkness and struggle in the experience of most serious Christians, and the more outstanding the spiritual genius, the more intense the gloom.

All in all, the combination of Christo-centricity, scholarly understanding, Church fellowship and pastoral guidance is as powerful as anything to defeat error. And it is unfortunate that to this day more Christians do not avail themselves of it, but are content to trust solely to a private and untrained judgement in seeking to unravel the intricacies of Scripture and of Divine Providence.

PREACHING AND COMMENTARY

The foregoing explains why preaching was considered by the Puritans to be so vital, why it was expository preaching with a bias toward 'practical divinity', and why it was so often taken down and published or issued as Biblical Commentary. John Owen says that from the decease of the original and especially-inspired preachers and writers of Scripture, God has called men 'to declare by writing what their apprehensions were, and what understanding God has given them in and about the sense of Scripture—Origen was the first, whose fooleries and mistakes

[46] 'The Lord has more truth and light yet to break forth out of his holy word', from J. Robinson's Farewell Address to the Pilgrim Fathers, accepted as reasonably authentic by Nuttall, p. 24, n.3.

[47] cf. H. Talon, *John Bunyan*, p. 57, and the whole section for a fine account of Bunyan's struggles; cf. R. H. Coats, *Types of English Piety*, pp. 86 ff. (London, 1912).

occasioned by the prepossession of his mind with *platonical philosophy*, confidence of his own great abilities (which indeed were singular and admirable), with the curiosity of a speculative mind, discouraged not others from endeavouring with more sobriety and better success to write entire expositions on some parts of the Scripture'.[48] If the commentator's task was, for Owen, rather like Socratic method in philosophy, a taking to the oars when the wind no longer filled the sails, it was as valuable a labour as any in God's Church. And John Smith or Smyth the Se-Baptist, though he would have yielded nothing to the Cambridge Puritans' conception of the Ministry, went so far as to say that many a paraphrase and commentary could express more of the meaning of the original than a bare translation could possibly do.[49]

Puritan preachers and commentators have certain distinguishing characteristics. One is the thoroughness with which they dwell on each word and phrase of the passage they are expounding, as though every grain of gold must be wrested from the heavenly mine. John Owen's exposition of the Epistle to the Hebrews takes him four folio volumes! Another is their fondness for divisions and subdivisions, which made them 'plain and perspicuous' in their generations, in contrast with the florid style of Andrewes, for instance, but which may daunt a modern reader. The published works of Perkins and Dod and Ames are illustrated with diagrams. Robert South's caricature of Puritan preaching descends to the abusive, but part of it is near enough to the truth to be worth quoting:

First of all they seize upon some Text, from whence they draw something (which they call a doctrine). . . . In the next place, being thus provided, they branch it into several heads; perhaps twenty or thirty or upwards. Whereupon, for the prosecution of these, they repair to some trusty concordance, which never fails them, and by the help of that, they range six or seven Scriptures under each Head; which Scriptures they prosecute one by one. . . .[50]

What South ignores is the reasonableness of the Puritan appeal. Like St Paul, the Puritans always imagined an objector at their elbow, and they attempted to answer him faithfully; like St Paul

---

[48] *Works*, IV.228.
[49] cf. W. H. Burgess, *John Smith the Se-Baptist*, p. 127.
[50] Cited Charles Smyth, *The Art of Preaching*, pp. 138-9.

too, they dealt with the great and numinous themes of the Faith and of their own experience, and this often fills with power their tedious paradigms.

THE SCRIPTURES FULFILLED

It is when we turn away from the folios to the spiritual biographies of Puritan saints and their works of spiritual direction that we see the most vital consequences of all this reading and preaching and comment. The Scriptures were to be re-lived in the life of the believer. Every Puritan biographer, every preacher of panegyric, fits his subject into a scriptural frame. Robert Bolton's biographer—to take an example almost at random—is acquainted with the Fathers both ancient and Protestant, and quotes them, but it is Scripture which illumines the crises of Bolton's life. The place of his birth (Blackburn) is remembered because 'God loves the very ground his servants tread on: The Lord shall count (says David) when he writeth up the people that this man was borne there'. His conversion is as violent as Job's torments or Paul's falling to the ground. His friendship with the writer was like that of Paul and Timothy, and in his last lengthy sickness, he submits to the divine will like David, or like Paul content to stay with his people below, though longing to be dissolved and be with Christ.[51]

When Paul Baynes writes to console the bereaved, he takes them straight to Ephrah and Rachel dying in childbed, or to Moriah where Abraham was almost parted from his beloved son. The tears of the childless are those of Anna, and the afflictions of Job are a constant consolation to the struggling Christian.[52] The onrush of death comes, according to William Perkins, like that of the fiery serpents in the wilderness; 'even so when any man feels death to draw neere, and his fiery sting to pierce the hearte, he must fixe the eye of a true and lively faith upon Christ exalted, and be crucified on the crosse, which being done he shall by death enter eternall life'.[53] Supremely, there is the Pilgrim's Progress of John Bunyan, which describes the whole of Christian life as a journey, with many of its landmarks the scenes and events of the Bible. Here indeed we observe both the similarity and the differ-

---

[51] *The Life and Death of Mr Bolton*, by E. B. Esq., Preface to *Workes*.
[52] P. Baynes' *Christian Letters* (1628 edn), unpaginated, unnumbered.
[53] W. Perkins's *Workes*, I.611.

ence between Puritan and medieval piety, for the scheme of this
book is a common-place of popular religious literature from the
fourteenth century onward, and Henri Talon summarizes the
work of many scholars in showing the secular sources of the
story.[54] But 'the popular imagery is tinged with the Bible. Job
felt the shadow of death weighing upon him, and the Psalmist
wandered in the dark valley: David trembled before the "quag"
and Jeremiah knew that "wilderness a land of pits . . . a land of
drought and of the shadow of death". . . . Thus with Bunyan
the Bible invades popular legend and transforms it.'[55] This was
almost a reversal of the medieval process, for there, popular
legend invaded the Bible; for the Puritans, the whole of life was
lived as a fulfilment of the Scriptures.

Two recent writers have shown that no Puritan thought of his
life more in scriptural terms than did Oliver Cromwell. His
speeches, letters, conversation and acts of policy were couched in
the words and phrases of the Bible.[56] It is in the Lord Protector's
career that we see some of the disadvantages which we have
already had cause to mention. It is almost impossible for people
of a later age not to feel, with Walter Scott in *Woodstock*, that there
is something hypocritical about the constant use of Scripture
language, and Dr Robert Paul has shown that Cromwell's ethics
in war may have been too much influenced by blood-thirsty Old
Testament precedents.[57] Even more of a problem is the fact that
in Cromwell's strange and tortured career the Scriptures did not
seem to be fulfilled, and the destiny to which he believed with all
his heart that the living God of the Bible had called him was
tragically clouded. Perhaps the Puritan sometimes failed sufficiently to unite Scripture with human reason, and perhaps he did
not always relate his own believed vocation, as the Bible does, to
that of the people of God, or interpret the promises eschatologic-
ally, as we have been taught to do. Nevertheless, the recapitulation of the Bible history in the believer's experience made God real,
and made both blessing and suffering contingent upon the divine

[54] *John Bunyan*, pp. 172 ff; cf. G. R. Owst, *Literature and Pulpit*, pp. 104-5.

[55] H. Talon, ibid, pp. 174-5.

[56] W. Haller, *Liberty and Reformation*, pp. 211 ff. R. S. Paul, *The Lord Protector*, esp.
App. 2, biblical analysis of Cromwell's letter to Mrs St John.

[57] ibid., p. 389. For an illustration of the 'Old Testament mentality' see L. Bayly,
Practice of Piety, pp. 198-9, where a fire at Tiverton is explained as the visitation of
the Divine Wrath in consequence of a Sunday market.

ordinance. The people of God in the wilderness, patriarchs and prophets, were the companions of the Puritan's way. He lived with them as intimately as the Catholic with his saints, and the Bible also gave to the Puritan his particular understanding of the Church and Sacraments.

This is a great mystery; but I speak concerning Christ and the Church.

EPHESIANS 5³²

He which hath said of the one sacrament 'wash and be clean' hath said concerning the other 'eat and live'. If therefore without any such particular and solemn warrant as this is, that poor distressed woman coming unto Christ for health, could so constantly resolve herself 'may I but touch the skirt of his garment I shall be whole', what moveth us to argue of the manner how life should come by bread? Our duty being here but to take what is offered, and most assuredly to rest persuaded of this, that can we but eat we are safe. . . . What these elements are in themselves it skilleth not; it is enough that to me which take them they are the body and blood of Christ; his promise in witness hereof sufficeth; his word he knoweth which way to accomplish; why should any cogitation possess the mind of a faithfull communicant but this? O my God thou art true; O my soul thou art happy!

RICHARD HOOKER

CHAPTER THREE

CHURCH AND SACRAMENTS

OUR forefathers were by no means all so preoccupied with the doctrine of the Church as theologians have been during the past two decades. In the Middle Ages, the doctrine received little prominence. The distinguished French Catholic, Emile Mersch, admits that the earlier medieval period was not a great age for the doctrine of Church, and that the later scholastics spoke of the Mystical Body with moderation.[1] St Bernard of Clairvaux has much to say about the Bride of Christ, but his references to the Body are few, and although the figure is implied in his sermons, he nowhere develops or expounds it.[2] The absence of systematic treatment in St Thomas Aquinas is sometimes a puzzle to his modern disciples.[3] John Wyclif, John Hus and Cardinal de Turrecremata (better known, if more notorious, as John Torquemada, the Inquisitor) wrote at length on the Church, but there is little else in the later Middle Ages, and 'even during Reformation times this subject received less detailed treatment than others'.[4]

This did not mean either that Protestants neglected it entirely or that their view of Christian salvation was guilty of that 'atomic individualism' which is one of our new deadly sins. Polemics do not always assist sound doctrinal statement, and we must agree that Protestant and Puritan reaction from Rome was sometimes too violent, though the Papacy was the chief abomination.[5] The Puritans in particular tended to repudiate the idea of the

---

[1] *The Whole Christ*, pp. 414, 451.

[2] *Pace* Thomas Merton, *The Sign of Jonas*, p. 40, who claims that Mersch does not do full justice to Bernard but supplies no evidence. A Bernadine authority tells me that Piszter's *Chrestomathia Bernardina* has nothing on the mystical Body.

[3] e.g. E. L. Mascall asks: 'But where even in St Thomas shall we find an adequate discussion of the mystical Body itself?' (*Corpus Christi*, p. 36).

[4] H. F. Woodhouse, *Doctrine of the Church*, p. 1.

[5] e.g. William Gouge's cheap onslaught on Hildebrand as 'a very brand of hell' (*Workes*, I.6, margin.) But this prejudice did not colour the Puritans' whole attitude to the Pre-Reformation Church.

Church as an authority.[6] But this did not lead to a denial either of the Church's divine origin or of its Catholicity. 'The Church of God is Catholike not Roman Catholike,' said Thomas Adams, and singled out the right ministration of the Sacraments and sincere preaching as its 'infallible mark'.[7] The word Catholic is frequently used in Puritan writings and always claimed for themselves. 'The Papists will say we forsake them, and not they us. We forsake them in the wall they us in the foundation.'[8] Owen declares that the Church as evidenced by Rome is not a divine institution at all.[9] But that the Church in the Old and New Testaments is necessary to salvation and that God Himself intended it no Puritan has any doubt. 'When God of old erected his worship, and enjoined the solemn observation of it, he also appointed a Church as his institution for the due celebration of it.'[10] As Eve was taken from the side of Adam, so 'Christ was nailed on the crosse and his most precious blood was shed, and out of it arise and spring all true Christians'.[11] And so, says Perkins: 'Whosoever is out of it (the Church) is also forth of the number of God's children, and he cannot have God for his Father, which hath not the Church for his mother.'[12]

Admittedly Perkins starts badly when he begins to expound the clause of the Creed about the Holy Catholic Church. Following various authorities,[13] he accepts the preposition 'in' only for those clauses of the Creed which are concerned with the Persons of the Blessed Trinity. We cannot believe *in* the Church as we believe *in* God, for this would be to commit ourselves to the creature as we

[6] e.g. J. Owen: 'There is . . . no need of the authority of any Churches' (*Divine Originall*, p. 44). R. Sibbes: 'They (our adversaries) say we must believe . . . because of the church. I say no. The church we believe hath a kind of working here but that is in the last place. For God himself in his word, he is the chief' (*Works*, III.374). These Puritans, however, were moving toward a more 'Independent' conception of the Church.

[7] *Workes* (1630), p. 557.

[8] R. Greenham, *Workes*, p. 273.

[9] J. Owen, *Works*, XV.224 ff. Anglicans took a more moderate view, see Woodhouse, *Doctrine of the Church*. Baxter did not unchurch the Romans and at the time of the Jansenist controversy many Puritans saw a new hope and a light in the darkness.

[10] Owen, ibid., XV.480. Perkins declares that the Church has existed ever since Eden (*Workes*, p. 371).

[11] W. Perkins, *Workes*, p. 361; cf. W. Gouge, *Domestical Duties*, *Workes* II, p. 54, and Tertullian, *De Animo*, 43: 'For as Adam was a figure of Christ, Adam's sleep shadowed out the death of Christ, who was to sleep a mortal slumber that from the wound inflicted on his side, might in like manner be typified the Church and true mother of the living.'

[12] op. cit., p. 342.

[13] e.g. Calvin, *Inst.*, IV.1, 2., following Augustine, etc.

may to the Creator alone; we can believe the Church as we accept human testimony. But since, to substantiate this, he quotes Augustine to the effect that believing in God means incorporation into His members, and since he goes on to describe in Pauline phrases the Church as the Body of Christ and therefore Christ Himself, the logic of his denial seems somewhat dubious.[14] But its intention will appear before we are done.

Canon Charles Smyth once said: 'For the high Calvinist, the determining doctrine was election by God in his transcendant sovereignty, whereas for the high Anglican, it was Sacramental union with Christ incarnate in his Mystical Body.'[15] The truth is that the Puritans held both doctrines together, as Perkins's definition of the Church makes plain: 'The Church is a peculiar companie of men predestinate to life everlasting and made one in Christ.'[16]

Perkins begins with the Divine Election. Predestination is the efficient cause of the Church, union its 'very forme ... whereby all that believe are made one with Christ'. His discussion reveals quite startlingly that the error of the doctrine of predestination is not in itself, but in the fact that its consequences were stated with such ruthless logic. Much error, indeed, arises from the human desire to make all mystery simple and ignore the antinomies of faith by which human thought must so often acknowledge its bounds. Double predestination is the disaster. 'It is a part of the counsell of God, whereby he hath before all times purposed in himselfe to shew mercie on some men, and to passe by others, shewing his justice on them for the manifestation of the glory of his own name.' That God's mercy and justice should be considered as operating as separate actions embodied in distinct decrees is almost incredible. As if all His purposes to all men were not at once both merciful and just! Yet the doctrine does answer the problem of the few professed Christians over against the many indifferent—a problem acute a few decades after the Reformation, when, says Perkins, in spite of the unhampered preaching of the true Gospel, there was no widespread repentance.

Of course, Perkins's exposition removes much of the sting of the

---

[14] *Workes*, pp. 342-3. Perkins quotes Augustine, *Tract. 29 in Joh.*, and Paul, Col. 1[18] and Gal. 3[16].

[15] Charles Smyth, 'The Cambridge Puritans', *Cambridge Review*, 1st February 1947, p. 269; cf. the composite pamphlet, *Catholicity* (1947), p. 27.

[16] All quotations from Perkins on the Creed, *Workes*, pp. 342 ff.

opening statement. Predestination concerns means as well as ends. No man is saved apart from God's call, justifying grace, and holy ordinances; and no man is condemned but for actual sins. It is not for individuals or even for the Church, except in most extraordinary circumstances, to pronounce damnation. The Gospel must be preached to all, and Christians must pray rather for the conversion than the confusion of the enemies of God. The great uses of predestination are to show that there cannot be justification by works, and to deliver Christians from all fears, whether inspired by astrologers or persecutors! 'Nowe then that we may have comfort in distress and something to stay upon in all our troubles; we in this world are as strangers in a far country; our passage homeward is over the sea of this world; the ship wherein we sail is the Churche; and Satan stirres up many blasts of troubles and temptations and his purpose is to sink the shippe or to drive it on the rocke; but we must take the anchor of hope and fasten it in heaven upon the foundation of God's election; which being done we shall passe in safety and rejoice in the midest of all stormes and tempests.' Our hope can never be in our-selves, for we have to recognize that there are those in hell not worse than us. It will always be a mystery why *we* have been saved.

This, be it noted, is the Reformed alternative to the doctrine of Apostolic Succession. Here is the Church's continuity and divinity—in God's election. She is created and kept in being by God's sovereign mercy.[17] Therefore 'the members thereof, whether they be in heaven or on earth are distinguished from all other companies whatsoever'. They are the Church of pardoned sinners justified by faith in Christ alone. As William Gouge points out, it is Christ's Love which makes the Church delightful.[18]

If, however, Divine Election were the only truth about the Church in which the Puritans were interested, it could more reasonably be complained that they did not believe 'in the real and actual gift of the divine life to human nature'.[19] They took the Epistle to the Ephesians very seriously, and with its help,

---

[17] Of course, this could express itself through a continuity of order as a 'secondary cause', as Presbyterians would agree.

[18] *Workes*, II.30-1.

[19] This assertion about traditional Protestantism is made by Yves Congar, the French Dominican (*Divided Christendom*, p. 91), and is both quoted and re-emphasized by E. L. Mascall (*Christ, the Christian and the Church*, pp. 80-1, 112).

united the various scriptural metaphors about God's relationship with His people. God has chosen His people, that is, He has made His Covenant with them. This Covenant of Love can be compared, as the Prophets compared it, to a marriage. So the Church is Christ's Bride. But the Bride is beloved as the Bridegroom's own flesh; indeed the two are 'one flesh'. So the Church is Christ's Body.[20] The Puritans have as much to say about Mystical Union as about Divine Election in their doctrine of the Church. 'It is not first actually a Church and afterward made Partaker of Union and Communion with Christ, but because it is united to Christ, therefore it is the Church of Christ.'[21] The adjective 'Mystical', which is very unpopular with modern Protestant theologians in this connexion, primarily means mysterious (from Ephesians 5^{32} etc.), and, secondarily, distinguishes the Church from the Body which walked in Galilee.[22]

Puritan writers do not hesitate to affirm the closeness of the Mystical Union. We are implanted into Christ by a lively, fruitful faith, says Robert Bolton, 'and blessedly knit unto Him by His Spirit, as fast as the sinews of His precious Body are knit unto his bones, His flesh to His sinewes and His skin to His flesh'.[23] So close is this union that not only is Jesus Himself called Christ, but so also are all the members together with Him. To belong to this Body is in itself the greatest privilege in the whole Universe, greater than to be a Prophet, Preacher or Apostle, more honourable than the Angels or the height of heaven.[24] No one warms to this theme so splendidly as Walter Marshal nearer the end of the seventeenth century. He asserts that union

---

[20] This is brought out clearly by W. Gouge, op. cit., II.42 ff.

[21] W. Ames, *Marrow of Divinity*, p. 314.

[22] e.g. W. Marshal, p. 43: 'I may well call this a mystical union because the apostle calleth it a mystery in an epistle full of mysteries'; cf. R. Bolton, *Directions*, p. 23, W. Gouge, *Workes*, II.52 f., 70 f. R. Sibbes, *Works*, I.12, W. Ames, op. cit. R. Hooker uses the word mystical in the same sense (*Laws of Ecclesiastical Polity*, V.67); cf. Columba Cary-Elwes, a modern Roman writer, *The Sheep and the Sheepfold* (1956), p. 143. Modern Protestant theologians do not seem to be convinced that the phrase 'Mystical Body' can thus be derived from Scripture, e.g. J. A. T. Robinson, *The Body* (1952), p. 52, A. R. George, *Communion with God*, pp. 248, 253. The term has caused confusion when divorced from Scripture. 'It is necessary to preserve the special use of the term *mystical body* to express the fact of the Body of Christ embracing both time and space' (*Ways of Worship* (London, 1951), pp. 337-8n.).

[23] *Directions*, p. 23.

[24] cf. W. Gouge, *Workes*, II.55. For the relation of Angels to the Church see W. Ames, op. cit., p. 135: 'The good Angells, altho' in some respects they pertaine to the Church by reason of that Union they have with Christ, and the grace of conservation communicated by him are not homogeneall members of the Church redeemed.'

with Christ is no mutual relation of separates. Christ is not our head in a mere political sense, as a King is head of a State. 'Christ liveth in me' does not mean that the individual is animated by some grace that Christ has wrought, but that he has become one flesh with Christ. This resembles the union between the Father and the Son, the Vine and the branches, the Bread and the eater. It is a great mystery. 'It is not only resembled but sealed in the Lord's Supper, where neither the Popish Transubstantiation, nor the Lutherans Consubstantiation, nor the Protestants Spiritual Presence of Christ's Body and Blood to the true Receivers can stand without it. . . . Though Christ be in Heaven and we on Earth, yet he can joyn our Souls and Bodies to his at such a distance, without any substantial change of either, by the same infinite Spirit dwelling in Him and us, and so our flesh will become his, when it is quickened by his Spirit, and his flesh ours as truly as if we did eat his flesh and drink his Blood, and he will be in us himself by his Spirit who is one with him, and who can unite us more closely to Christ than any material substance can do, or who can make a more close and intimate union betwixt Christ and us.'[25] This does not mean that there is any confusion of persons, or that we are absorbed into the Godhead, or that we are made immediately perfect. It is a union of Spirit. As Perkins says: 'The very same Spirit of God that dwelleth in the manhood of Christ, and filleth it with all graces above measure is derived thence, and dwelleth in all true members of the Church.' It is rather curious that Perkins does not make use of that long tradition of dogmatic theology, which teaches that the Holy Spirit is the bond of union of the Godhead. Thus the principle of the Church's union and of the union of the Blessed Trinity is the same.[26] However, Perkins is insistent that Christians are united to Christ and so to the whole Trinity. And it is whole Christ, God and man, who is really communicated to all those who are ordained to salvation. Like Marshal, Perkins regards the Lord's Supper as the proclamation of this, where 'expresse mention is made not only of Christ's merit but of his very body and blood, whereby the whole humanity is signified'. Christ is given us both by imputation and infusion. Thus we are justified by Christ's

[25] W. Marshal, *Gospel Mystery*, p. 44.
[26] cf. Augustine, *De Trinitate*; F. J. Hall, *Dogmatic Theology*, p. 273; and among seventeenth-century writers, J. Everard, *Gospel Treasury*, p. 107.

imputed righteousness, but holiness is wrought in our hearts by the Spirit 'as one Candle is lighted from another.'[27]

Holiness is only possible through union with Christ. All our ability to obey the law and do good works depends on our union with Christ in the Mystical Body. Sanctification is as much of grace as justification. Christ's incarnation, death and resurrection, says Marshal, 'were the cause of all the holiness that ever was, or shall be given to man, from the fall of Adam to the end of the world, and that by the mighty Power of his Spirit whereby all saints that ever were or shall be are joined together to be members of that one mystical Body whereof he is the Head'.[28] This seems to have an echo of Augustine who describes the Church which is Christ's Body as 'the whole race of saints, from Abel down to all those who ever will be born, and will believe in Christ until the end of the world, for all belong to one city'.[29]

But here we must pause. What is the precise relation of the Mystical Union of which the Puritans speak to the institutional Church in the world? Is the Church we enter by faith the same as the Church we enter by baptism? Perkins clearly sees Divine Predestination and Mystical Union as the foundation of the Holy Catholic Church which extends throughout all ages; but Thomas Adams says: 'The Catholic Church is always invisible, the members thereof only knowne to God';[30] and Marshal, later in his book, brings in Church fellowship and ordinances conventionally, as means of holiness—indispensable means it is true, but not, like Mystical Union, its very presupposition and root. Indeed, he has a phrase which is curious in the light of what has occurred earlier—'Wrath is denounced against those who are not members of it (the Church), at least of the Mystical Body'—but he does not refer back to what has gone before.[31] He nowhere specifically states that Church membership in itself means mystical union with Christ, and the words at the heart of his earlier discussion are significant: 'Believers are members of Christ's Body of his Flesh and of his Bones, and they two, Christ and the Church are one

[27] One does not want to bandy metaphors, but this figure of Perkins is an apt rejoinder to Mersch's charge that the Body for Protestants is like a lighted lamp which illumines but is opaque (*The Whole Christ*, p. 504).

[28] *Gospel Mystery*, p. 58.

[29] Augustine, *In Ps. XC Sermo 2*, No. 1; quoted by Mersch, *The Whole Christ*, p. 415, and E. L. Mascall, *Christ, the Christian and the Church*, p. 120.

[30] *Workes*, p. 557.

[31] op. cit., pp. 307-8.

flesh.'[32] Marshal is emphatic that the Protestant doctrine of
Faith and Free Grace does not destroy 'all diligent use of the
means of holiness and salvation', and breed up a company of
'Lazy Solifidians'.[33] But in his mind there is a distinction between
that union with Christ which is a gift of God appropriated by faith,
and the duties of Church membership which spring from it and
'realize' it but cannot of themselves bring it about. The believer
does not become a member of Christ by attending worship,
receiving the Sacrament, or associating with Christians. Only God
incorporates him into Christ. To be in Christ is to be in the
Church, but no external practices of institutional religion divorced
from faith in the Pauline sense can bring us into that relationship.
There may even be those who are members of the Church only
before men; and as Perkins points out, there are times of almost
universal apostasy when the true Church lies hidden from mortal
sight.

It is not felt today that the distinction between the visible and
the invisible Church is particularly helpful, but it does correspond
to the tension of history. William Ames defines it scholastically as
'A distinction of the adjuncts of the same subject, because in-
visibility is an affection or manner of the Church in respect of the
essentiall, and internall forme, visibility is an affection or manner
of the Church in respect of the accidentall and outward forme'.[34]
There are not two Churches, but different modes of the one.
This one Church never wholly ceases to be visible even amid
impurities of form and worship. Outside its Divine Life there is
no salvation, and the gates of hell cannot prevail against it.

It is when he is thinking of this part of the paradox that Perkins
hesitates to say that we can believe *in* the Church as we believe in
God. On earth the Church is 'a mixt company', the Body of
Christ's humiliation as well as of his glory.[35] As Baxter says: 'In
the meantime the Church though black is yet comely in the eyes of
Christ and of all that see by the light of his spirit. And our tender-
hearted Saviour disdaineth not to be the physician of such an
hospital as hath many sorts of diseases in it, and many of them very
great.'[36] This figure of the Church as a hospital—which seems

---

[32] op. cit., p. 43.   [33] ibid., p. 267.   [34] *Marrow of Divinity*, p. 137.
[35] cf. T. F. Torrance, *S.J.T.*, II.250; J. A. T. Robinson, *The Body*, pp. 74-5.
[36] *Works*, XVI.307; cf. ibid., XXII.160: 'The Church on earth is a mere hospital',
but there he is thinking chiefly of the calamities of the time. The Scripture reference
is Canticles I.5.

to have originated with Augustine—is also found in Richard Sibbes, pleading like Baxter for mutual wisdom and meekness: 'The Church of Christ is a common hospital wherein all are in some measure sick of some spiritual disease or another.'[37] Thomas Goodwin declares that not all the Pauline hope for the Church is as yet fulfilled.[38] But the Puritans, conscious as they were of the errors of the Church on earth, were not blind to the glories of that great Church with which she is one, to which her membership gives entrance, and where Christ is all in all, and the spirits of just men are made perfect.

THE SEALS OF THE COVENANT

We have already quoted Walter Marshal's statement that the Mystical Union is not only resembled but sealed in the Lord's Supper. The metaphor of the seal is scriptural, and is found in Calvin. Bullinger takes over and applies to the Lord's Supper a distinction, that most likely originated with Zwingli, between a piece of wax and a seal stamped with the Royal Arms. The bread and wine of the Sacrament are as the King's seal. This has been criticized on the ground that the seal is still only a sign.[39] The Puritans would not have been impressed by this contention. For William Ames there is a profound difference between 'bare signs' and signs which seal. 'A seale is that which not merely representeth, but also exhibiteth by sealing.'[40] A Royal seal is a sign which conveys the power and purpose of the King. It takes on the character of what it conveys. Thus the sacred elements which seal to the faithful the Covenant of Grace and their Union with Christ are no common signs but of the most august and numinous quality.

Thomas Manton declares that the sacraments give us 'a great advantage over the bare word and proposal of the Covenant'.[41] 'The word speaks to all promiscuously, as inviting; the sacraments to everyone in particular as obliging.' Manton compares the

---

[37] *Works*, I.57.
[38] *Works*, I.521.
[39] Charles Smyth, *Cranmer and the Reformation under Edward VI*, p. 104.
[40] *Marrow of Divinity*, p. 163. The Puritans are fond of an analogy of Augustine's which Aquinas repeats. The elements are representations just as when we say of a picture, 'That is Cicero' (Augustine, *Ep*.23, Aquinas, *Summa Theol.*, Part III Q83, Ic, 73, 5c.; cf. H. Smith, *Works*, I.59, R. Vines, a *Treatise of Lord's Supper*, pp. 104-5, etc.).
[41] *How Ought we to Improve our Baptism*, reprinted in *The Morning Exercises at St Giles, Cripplegate* (1844 edn), p. 94.

word to the brazen serpent to which the afflicted might look and live; the sacraments are like the blood which the Children of Israel were bidden sprinkle on their door-posts, the guarantee of God's mercy, appropriated by the faithful in obedience to His command. When Christ says to the recipient 'This is my body', there is a solemn investiture of the believer into all the privileges purchased by Christ's crucified body.

The Puritans frequently use the scriptural word 'exhibit' in connexion with the sacraments. They stress the *visibility* of the rites. The mysteries of godliness are laid before our eyes. Thomas Manton even suggests that God chose the senses of seeing and hearing as the means of conveying His Grace in preference to the grosser feeling, smelling, and tasting! It is somewhat curious that he should say this of the Lord's Supper. He obviously will have no carnal interpretation of the Command, 'Take, eat!', or of the Johannine 'Except ye eat the flesh of the Son of Man and drink his blood ye have no life in you'. Christ's word alone is effective, and it is visibly set forth in the signs which recall the act of our redemption.[42]

The sacraments are ordinances of the Church. Like Circumcision and the Passover under the Old Covenant, Baptism and the Lord's Supper have no meaning outside the life of the people of God. Here 'is the seat of the administration of this ordinance (the Lord's Supper) wherein we have such peculiar and intimate communion with Christ, . . . in the Church we have all this treasure'.[43] Richard Greenham insists that Baptism must be a public act in the congregation. William Ames will have the

---

[42] *The Morning Exercises at St Giles, Cripplegate*, p. 95; cf. 1 Cor. 11[26]; cf. also a verse from a Eucharistic hymn of Charles Wesley's:

> Crucified before our eyes,
> Where we our Maker see.

(*Poetical Works*, III.230, 'Hymns on the Lord's Supper', No. 21; *MHB* (1933), No. 191).

There is an interesting comparison and contrast between this and some lines from Gerard Manley Hopkins's translation of Aquinas's *Adoro te devote*:

> Seeing, touching, tasting are in thee deceived;
> How says trusty hearing? that shall be believed;
> What God's Son hath told me, take for true I do;
> Truth himself speaks truly or there's nothing true.

[43] J. Owen, *Works*, IX.528; cf. H. de Lubac (*Catholicism*, p. 35), who quotes a German to the effect that the causality of the sacraments is to be found not so much 'in a paradoxical efficacy in the supernatural order of a rite or perceptible action as in the existence of a society which under the appearance of a human institution hides a divine reality'; and then goes on to say: 'All the Sacraments are essentially Sacraments of the Church; in her alone do they produce their full effect.'

sacraments administered only by lawfully appointed ministers and only in the assembly of the Church.[44]

Once this is granted, however, the problem arises of the fencing of tables. The Puritans repudiated the idea of the Lord's Supper as a converting ordinance. Richard Baxter states categorically, 'God never commanded any infidel to receive it to his conversion', though he believes it may be blessed to the conversion of hypocrites. Even so, no hypocrite should come to the Sacrament in the hope that it may convert him; rather should he first repent and believe, and accept the covenant of God. Then may he come to seal the covenant.[45] Richard Vines does not deny that a man may be converted at the Supper, but the ordinance was not appointed for that purpose. Its whole symbolism suggests the welcome to the Father's house and nourishment of souls already converted.[46]

This was deemed by John Wesley, a century later, to be 'a gross falsehood',[47] and there are many accounts in early Methodist literature of conversions at the Lord's Table, although some cases like that of Wesley's own mother testify more to the receipt of a new assurance of God's love and pardon by a faithful penitent than to the transformation of reprobates. Moreover Wesley had to enforce certain rules to maintain the sanctity of the ordinance.[48] Much depends on what precisely is meant by 'conversion'.

BAPTISM

This understanding of the relation of the sacraments to the Church and the Covenant was one reason why our Puritans maintained the validity of Infant Baptism. Unless the New Covenant extends to infants, it is narrower than the old; for children were circumcised. Ames sees in Paul's linking of the 'circumcision not made with hands' with Baptism, clear evidence that Christian Baptism was instituted as the counterpart and fulfilment of Jewish circumcision.[49] It is to be administered but once, and is for all to whom the Covenant belongs.

But there was an even deeper reason why men like Ames

---

[44] R. Greenham, *Workes*, p. 187; W. Ames, *Marrow of Divinity*, p. 181.
[45] *Works*, V.408.
[46] *Treatise of Lord's Supper*, pp. 247-57; cf. S. Charnock, *Works*, IV.484: 'The supper seems not to be a renewing, converting ordinance.'
[47] *Journal*, II.361.
[48] See J. C. Bowmer, *The Sacrament of the Lord's Supper in Early Methodism*, p. 110.
[49] *Marrow of Divinity*, p. 182; Colossians, 2[11-12].

contended for Infant Baptism. Man is passive in the beginning of regeneration, and infants 'are as capable of this Sacrament in respect of the chiefe use of it, as these of age are. . . . Faith and repentance doe no more make the Covenant of God now than in the time of Abraham (who was the Father of the Faithfull) therefore the want of those acts ought no more to hinder baptisme from infants now, than it did forbid circumcision then.'[50]

Baptism was regarded as the essential preliminary to receiving the Lord's Supper. Thomas Manton interprets the Lord's words to Peter at the foot-washing as a reference to the Sacraments: 'If I wash thee not (i.e. baptism) thou hast no part with me (i.e. the Lord's Supper).'[51] There is, however, neither magic nor 'natural virtue' in Baptism. 'It is,' says William Gouge, 'no physical or natural means of working grace, as if the grace which is sealed up thereby were inherent in the water or the Minister's act of sprinkling it (as in medicines, herbs, salves, meats and the like; there is inherent that virtue that proceedeth from the use of them and being applied they have their operation whether a man believe it or no) but it is only a voluntary instrument which Christ useth as it pleaseth him to work what grace or measure of grace seemeth best to him'.[52] Walter Marshal warns against sacramental superstition: 'Beware also of making an Idol of Baptism and putting it in the place of Christ, as the Papists do who hold that it confereth grace by the very work that is performed in the administration of it. And as many ignorant people do that trust rather on their baptism than on Christ.'[53] This was why the

[50] *Marrow of Divinity*, p. 183; cf. the vigorous words of Bernard Manning: 'In baptism the main thing is not what men do but what God has done. It is a sign that Christ claims all men as His own and that he has redeemed them to a new way of life. That is why we baptize children. We do not baptize them because we or they have faith. . . . Every time we baptize a child, we declare to the whole world in the most solemn manner that God does for us what he does without our merits and even without our knowledge' (*Why not abandon the Church?* (London, 1939), pp. 47-8).

Henry Lawrence (1600-62), a lay-man, regards sacraments as acted parables which demand faith for their understanding. Thus a sacrament must always follow the Word, and be itself followed by a devout and holy life. He elucidates the baptismal signs— water represents cleansing from the guilt and stain of sin; dipping, for naturally Lawrence will have no sprinkling, symbolizes both the depth of the divine justice with which Christ for our sake was swallowed up, and the believers' death and burial with him. Staying in the water is a reminder of Christ's descent into hell. See his *Of Baptisme* (1646).

[51] *Improve our Baptism*, p. 96.

[52] *Workes*, II. 35.

[53] *Gospel Mystery*, pp. 284-5. He goes on to argue that to account all Baptism null and void except that administered to adults is to deny faith, since were infant baptism of no account we could be saved through faith.

sign of the Cross in Baptism was deplored. John Bunyan was so fearful of a new 'law of commandments contained in ordinances', that he regarded Baptism as a minor Sacrament compared with the Lord's Supper. Both Sacraments are 'made for us not we for them', but according to Bunyan the Supper only was a Church ordinance, 'for the Church as a Church'. Baptism is 'not commanded as a rule of strict obedience', and we have no clear scriptural guidance as to the receiving or rejecting of believers unbaptized.[54] This certainly was not the general belief of our authors, but they refused to consign the unbaptized to hell or limbo. Gouge castigated the Roman attitude as 'a mercilesse sentence without any warrant of God's word'.[55] God's promise is to the seed of the faithful, and not even the precious ordinances of scripture can limit the operation of the divine grace for those whom He has called.

The Puritans have much to say about 'improving' our baptism. Walter Marshal implores his readers to ask this question:

What good use do you make of your Baptism? How often or seldom do you think upon it? The vulgar sort of Christians, yea it may be feared many sincere Converts, do so little think upon their own Baptism and study to make due improvement of it, that its of no more profit to their Souls, than if they had never bin Baptized; yea, their sin is the more aggravated by rendring such an Ordinance of none effect to their Souls, through their own gross neglect. Tho Baptism be administered to us but once in our lives, yet we ought frequently to reflect upon it, and upon all Occasions to put the Question to ourselves Into what were we Baptised? Acts 19[2]. What this Ordinance Seals? What did it engage us to? And accordingly, we must stir up and strengthen ourselves by our Baptism, to lay hold on the Grace which it seals to us, and to fulfil its Engagements. . . . We should remember that our Baptism sealed our putting-on of Christ and our being the Children of God by Faith in Christ, and our being no longer under the former Schoolmaster the Law. Galatians 3[25-7]. And that it sealed to us the *putting off the body of sin* and our *Burial and Resurrection with Christ by Faith*, and the *forgiving of our trespasses*. Colossians 2[12-13]. Our being made *Members of one Body* of Christ and to *drink into one Spirit*. 1 Corinthians 12[13]. We may find by such things as these which are more fully discovered in the Gospel that it is the proper nature and

---

[54] J. Bunyan, 'Differences in Judgement about Water-Baptism—no Bar to Communion', *Works*, II.618 ff. For the attitude to the sacraments of those whom G. F. Nuttall calls the more radical Puritans, see Nuttall, pp. 90 ff.
[55] *Workes*, p. 36; cf. R. Greenham, *Workes*, pp. 187, 267-8.

tendency of Baptism to guide us to faith in Christ alone for the remission of Sins, Holiness and all salvation, by Union and Fellowship with him, and that a diligent improvement of this Ordinance must needs be of great advantage to the Life of Faith.[56]

There is no better opportunity for the improvement of Baptism than to share in its administration at the conclusion of public worship. Lewis Bayly exhorts the Churchgoer not to neglect this, and bids him participate by various suitable meditations. He must consider his own 'ingrafting into the visible body of Christ's Church'. Bayly continues: 'Repay thy debt in praying for the infant which is to be baptised (as other Christians did in the like case for thee) that God would give him the inward effects of Baptism by his blood and spirit . . . assist the Church in praising God for grafting another member into his Mystical Bodie . . . prove whether the effects of Christ's death killeth sin in thee, and whether thou be raised to newness of life by the virtue of his Resurrection . . . show thyself to be a free man of Christ's corporation, having a voice or consent in the admission of others into that holy society.'[57]

The Puritans considered that Baptism was a great ground of the believer's confidence. William Perkins regards the remembrance of the vows made on the Christian's behalf as powerful to restrain sin. Baptism is 'a board to swimme upon, when a man shall fear the shipwracke of his soule' and it helps him back to repentance when all might be lost.[58] Thomas Manton quotes the words with which Luther comforted himself when in despair: '*Ecce, baptizatus sum et credo in Christum crucifixum.*'[59]

THE DEVOUT UNDERSTANDING OF THE LORD'S SUPPER

The Puritans would have wholeheartedly endorsed Calvin's strictures against the Romans who 'deemed it sufficient if the priest muttered the formula of consecration, while the people looked stupidly on'.[60] The spate of sermons and manuals on the Eucharist throughout the seventeenth century bears witness to

---

[56] *Gospel Mystery*, pp. 285-7; cf. T. Manton, 'Improve our Baptism'; R. Sibbes, *Works*, VII.488 ff.
[57] *Practice of Piety*, pp. 215-16 (incorrectly 115).
[58] *Workes*, II.79.
[59] *Improve our Baptism*, p. 96.
[60] Calvin, *Inst.*, IV.xiv.4.

this.[61] The title, the Lord's Supper, which the Puritans preferred, is not only 'another indication of Puritan loyalty to the Word of God',[62] but also an evidence of their belief that the Sacrament is to be shared. No longer must people come to Mass merely to see and adore the Host, but to enter into full participation. Thus the worshippers need to be prepared as much as the minister. The favourite text of Puritan preachers on the Sacrament is: 'Let a man examine himself, and so let him eat of that bread and drink of that cup.'[63] Those who cannot come with understanding and self-examination are thus debarred—children, idiots, ignorant persons.[64] The Lord's Supper is a perpetual obligation. William Perkins writes: 'Everie man of yeares living in the Church, and being baptised is bound in conscience by God's commandment to use the Lord's Supper. In the Institution of the Supper, the Lord gave a Sacramentall word; whereof there be two partes; a commandment and a promise.'[65] John Owen is even more emphatic: 'And give me leave to say it, they that look towards Christ, and do not put themselves in the way of partaking this ordinance, they refuse the principal part of that profession which God calls them unto in this world. The truth is, we have been apt to content ourselves with a profession of moral obedience; but it is a profession of Christ's institution by which alone we glorify him in this world.'[66]

Like Calvin, and many early Separatists, our Puritans believed in frequent Communion.[67] We rub our eyes when we read Ignatius Loyola's rule that the Holy Sacrament be received, 'once a year, and much better every month, and much better still every eight days', and contrast it with William Perkins: 'Some there bee that thinke it sufficient to receive the Communion once by the yeare, namely at Easter time. Whereas, on the contrary, it is to be used as oft as may be; considering it is nothing but the shewing

---

[61] See e.g. W. W. Biggs, 'Preparation for Communion, a Puritan Manual', *Congregational Quarterly* (January 1954).

[62] Horton Davies, p. 205.

[63] 1 Cor 11^{28}. It would not be too much to claim that every Puritan Divine preached on this text. Henry Smith's second sermon on the Lord's Supper ends with the words: 'Now if you cannot remember all that I have said, yet remember the text, that is examine yourselves . . .' (*Works*, I.84).

[64] R. Greenham, *Workes*, p. 476; R. Baxter, *Works*, IV.320.

[65] *Workes*, II.81.

[66] *Works*, IX.527.

[67] *Inst.*, IV.17, 46; and Horton Davies, pp. 205 ff, especially his citation from the Latin letter of 1626 to Hans Ries, the representative of the Anabaptist Churches in Holland.

E

forth of the Lord's death till he come; which is not once or twice in the yeare, but often yea, continually to bee remembered.'[68] Presbyterians in England and Scotland, contrary to Calvin, preferred to esteem the Lord's Supper by infrequent celebrations, and normal Anglican practice was certainly not a weekly Eucharist; but although they always feared formality,[69] most Puritans believed with Baxter that the Table Fellowship of the Acts of the Apostles signified Communion in the Primitive Church each Lord's Day, and this all well-disciplined congregations should emulate.[70] Thus should Christians live 'continually in a state of general preparation'.[71]

There is of course the perennial problem of the recipient's worthiness. The sense of unfitness should not, however, beguile us from a duty appointed by God and ordained by Christ just before His death. The Lord's command is enough. From this point we can trace a two-fold emphasis in Puritan teaching:

(1) The Sacrament is by its very nature for sinners. 'If thou thoughte thyselfe fit,' says John Preston, 'thou shouldest not have it; even therefore because thou feelest thyself unfit, the rather thou shalt be received to mercy.'[72] Thus are the fears removed of

---

[68] *Workes*, II.81; cf. S. Charnock, *Works*, I.402 ff. Ignatius Loyola, *Spiritual Exercises*, 197.

[69] See e.g. R. Vines, *Treatise of Lord's Supper*, p. 173.

[70] R. Baxter, *Works*, IV.245-318; cf. Horton Davies, pp. 213-14; cf. Acts 2[42], 20[7]. Oscar Cullmann in *Urchristentum und Gottesdient* has argued that in the primitive Church there was an early tendency toward establishing worship at one place and on one day —a house on the first day of the week. The basic elements of the service were praise and prayer with the Eucharistic meal as the culminating point. Cullmann thinks that the early Eucharist was related to meals partaken with the Risen Lord, and that the association with the Last Supper and Passion was due to Paul. Be that as it may, Cullmann sees a weekly Eucharist behind such passages as Acts 2[42]. This obviously supports Calvin and the Puritans in the place they ascribe to the Eucharist in the early Church, even though, following the Western Tradition, they relate it more to Christ's death than to his Resurrection. Hans Lietzmann in *Messe und Herrenmahl* distinguishes two types in the primitive Eucharist, 'the breaking of bread' has no reference to the Last Supper; it is the continuance of the family meals, which, according to Jewish custom, Jesus celebrated with his disciples, and which the Jerusalem Church continued after his death in glad expectation of the Parousia.

[71] Further research is needed as to how often in practice Puritan congregations celebrated the Lord's Supper. The Westminster Assembly referred the question of frequency to the officials of each congregation. J. Wickham Legg quotes Restoration divines as lamenting an almost complete neglect of the Sacrament during the Commonwealth (*English Church Life, 1660-1833* (London, 1914), p. 21). But the prejudice of these men would make them exaggerate. I imagine that a study of such records as are available would reveal some divergence of custom, but a considerable faithfulness to the tradition of Perkins and the teaching of Baxter and Owen. Infrequent celebration would not necessarily mean a dishonouring of the Sacrament, but a greater solemnity in its preparation.

[72] *The Cuppe of Blessing*, p. 22.

those who have, as Baxter says, 'a deeper sense of the danger than of the benefit'.[73]

(2) Because we are unworthy, and yet God condescends to receive us, we should for ever strive to become worthy of the love which the Holy Supper proclaims. If our sense of sin makes us draw back from the Lord's Table, how dare we join in Christian prayer or any act of worship? If we are not ready to be forgiven, we are not ready for salvation at all. 'If you are not fit for this ordinance, you are not fit for heaven.'[74] The Sacrament is indeed the means of becoming fit.[75] The Sacrament was ordained, says Preston, so that 'when there is a decay of grace in your hearts, you may go to this fountaine and fill the Cisternes again to recover strength'.[76] The purpose of this Sacrament is 'to knit the knot stronger between Christ and us'.[77]

Mere devout feelings are adequate neither as a preparation for the Sacrament nor as a test of its efficacy. John Owen exposes the 'deceit' that 'where there is a disposition in the person, there needs no preparation for the duty'.[78] On the other hand, Perkins deals with the case of a man who 'after often receiving still doubteth whether he hath faith or no'. The very sorrow for sin and desire for Christ are sufficient to show that faith is begun. 'The poore beggar by the way side enjoyeth the almes that is given him, though he receive it with a lame and leprous hand. The stomacke that loathes physicke revives if it receives into it at the first but one drop of the potion prescribed, and that in very weake and fainting manner it will be able at length to take benefite by a greater quantitie, and in the meane time it receives good. The man that is in close prison if he sees but one little beam of the sunne by a small crevice; by that very beame he hath use of the Sunne, though he seeth not the whole body of the Sunne. In like manner, though our faith, the hand of our souls, be mingled with weaknesse and corruption, though we feele never so little measure of God's grace in us; yea, though our knowledge be never so small, yet it is an argument that the spirit of God begins

[73] *Works*, IV.283.
[74] S. Charnock, *Works*, p. 413; cf. Calvin's quotation from Chrysostom, *Inst.* IV.17, 45.
[75] S. Charnock, ibid., p. 414.
[76] *A Preparation to the Lord's Supper*, p. 115.
[77] ibid., pp. 117-18.
[78] *Works*, p. 553.

to worke in our hearts and that we have by God's mercy begun to lay hold on Christ.' The final comfort of the doubting soul is this, 'that though hee doe not apprehend Christ, yet Christ apprehendeth and accepteth him'.[79] Yet this Sacrament, like Baptism, must afterwards be improved.[80]

The Puritans, after the manner of the devotional writers of the Middle Ages, prescribe at length the devotional thoughts which should attend each act and moment of the Service. Henry Smith speaks for many when he says: '. . . when we see the minister take the bread to feed us, we may conceive that Christ, being God from everlasting, took our flesh to save us. When we see the minister give the bread to our hand, we must conceive that Christ as truly offereth himself to our faith to be received of us.'[81] Similarly in the composite manual, *A Garden of Spirituall Flowers*, the reader is bidden to meditate at the delivery of Bread and Wine 'as if with thine owne eyes thou diddest then behold his body nailed to the Crosse, and his precious bloud shed for thy sake'.

We must notice particularly four characteristics of Puritan Sacramental teaching.

(1) *The Lord's Supper is related to Redemption rather than to Creation*

The present-day 'Liturgical Movements' in Roman, Anglican and Reformed Churches lay considerable stress on the offering of bread and wine at Holy Communion, fruits of nature's bounty and man's toil, symbols of the whole complex of natural and human relationships. Puritanism regards the milled wheat and crushed grapes rather as signs of the sufferings which human sin inflicted upon the Saviour. 'Seeing there is such a nature in the creatures that the outward things have suffered many injuries before they became good food, as the corne being cutte downe in its perfite age, pressed out of his husks with the flaile, losing all his intralles with the violence of the Mill, and after passing through the parching heate of the Oven is made good bread; so the flesh of Jesus Christ went under many paines, and the

[79] W. Perkins, *Workes*, II.83-4.
[80] See Baxter, *Works*, IV.285.
[81] *Works*, I.47; cf., Perkins, *Works*, p. 83; Sibbes, *Works*, IV.68 ff; Baxter, *Works*, IV.336 (in great detail); L. Bayly, *The Practice of Piety*, pp. 265-70; cf. also Bishop Beveridge, quoted H. R. McAdoo, *The Structure of Caroline Moral Theology*, p. 140. This is medieval, except that those devotions were to accompany Mass in Latin. See G. Dix, *The Shape of the Liturgy*, pp. 605 ff.

blood of Christ as the grape in its most flourishing estate was
pressed out of the veines, and sustained hard passions, and shall
nothing of us suffer with him?'[82] There is no Great Entrance in
Puritan, or indeed in Protestant, tradition.[83] Yet there is a hint
in Baxter of the linking of the elements with creation: 'When you
look on the bread and wine which is provided and offered for this
holy use, remember that it is the Creator of all things on whom
you live. . . .'[84] But this is to be a reminder of sin, of the violation
of natural law. John Owen declares that in taking bread and
wine God took the 'cream of the creation: which is an endless
storehouse, if pursued, of representing the mysteries of Christ'.[85]
But Joseph Stennett, the Baptist to whom belongs the distinction
of having published in 1697 the first collection of Eucharistic
Hymns, shows us whither this contemplation of nature leads:

> Lord, all the works thy hand has formed
> In earth and heaven above
> And all thy tracks of providence
> Show thee a God of love.

> But thy surprising acts of grace
> To Adam's guilty seed
> Loudly proclaim to all the world
> That God is love indeed.[86]

These undistinguished stanzas are but the herald of what Isaac
Watts was to write. Modern theologians have sought to make us
aware that in the sacraments Nature participates in the process of
salvation,[87] but nowhere is there more majestic expression of the

---

[82] Greenham, *Workes*, p. 430; cf. Charnock, *Works*, p. 397, Sibbes, *Works*, IV.66.
This view is also found in Daniel Brevint, whose *Christian Sacrament and Sacrifice* Charles
Wesley paraphrases in his *Hymns on the Lord's Supper* (*Poetical Works*, III.216). No. 2
begins:

> In this expressive bread I see
> The wheat by man cut down for me,
>   And beat, and bruised, and ground:
> The heavy plagues, and pains, and blows,
> Which Jesus suffer'd from His foes,
>   Are in this emblem found.

Cf. Evelyn Underhill's poem 'Corpus Christi' for a modern Catholic expression of
this.
[83] cf. A. R. George, *S.J.T.*, IV.ii.157 ff.
[84] *Works*, IV.336.
[85] *Works*, IX.540.
[86] *Works*, IV, *Hymns for the Lord's Supper*, No. 25.
[87] e.g. Paul Tillich, *The Shaking of the Foundation* (London, 1949), p. 86.

relation between Nature and Grace than in this Communion Hymn:

> *Nature with open volume stands*
> *To spread her Maker's praise abroad;*
> *And every labour of his hands*
> *Shows something worthy of a God.*

> *But in the grace that rescued man*
> *His brightest form of glory shines;*
> *Here on the Cross 'tis fairest drawn*
> *In precious blood and crimson lines.*[88]

(2) *The Lord's Supper is related to the Sacrifice of Calvary*

The Puritan preoccupation with redemption allows Vines to say that the Supper exhibits Christ in but one of His aspects, though that the most precious, i.e. as dying.[89] He will have no reference to the Resurrection and Ascension in the Sacrament. It is thus that he rejects 'the Romish trick of Concomitancy', whereby laymen are denied the cup. Since it is the Lord's death that is shown forth and not His glorified Body brought down from Heaven, the argument that the virtue of His blood belongs as much to the Bread as the Cup is absurd. The Puritans are therefore extreme examples of the Western tradition, and of the Pauline emphasis.

Yet reaction from the Roman Mass naturally made the Puritans cautious in the use of sacrificial language about the Eucharist. There can be no repetition of what was done once for all on Calvary, and, as Owen says, the whole glory of the Sacrament is in the work which a triumphant Saviour has finished for man: 'He does not tender himself as one that *can* do these things (it is a relief when we have an apprehension that Christ can do all this for us); nor does he tender himself as one that *will* do these things upon any such conditions as shall be prescribed unto us; but he tenders himself unto our faith as one that *hath* done these things.'[90] The Lord's Supper is the means whereby we avail ourselves of the one sacrifice of the Cross. It is, says Vines, the sacrifice of Christ eaten and drunk, i.e. appropriated by us.[91] Says Owen: 'The sacrifice is offered; Christ—God's Passover; God makes a feast upon it, and invites his friends to sit down at his

---

[88] Isaac Watts, *Hymns and Sacred Songs* (1731 edn), III.10.
[89] *Treatise of Lord's Supper*, p. 8.   [90] *Works*, p. 565.   [91] *Treatise of Lord's Supper*, p. 14-15.

table there being now no difference between him and us.'[92]
Further than this the Puritans did not go; but in using the Epistle
to the Hebrews to interpret the Eucharist, the way is open to
relate our worship here to the perfect sacrifice of the Cross. We
do not, cannot, repeat that sacrifice, but through the Eucharist
on earth we share in the offering which our great High Priest
and Intercessor presents eternally anew in Heaven.

(3) *There is a reverent agnosticism about the precise manner of Christ's
sacramental presence*

John Owen speaks for many when he says: 'It is a great mystery,
and great wisdom and exercise of faith lie in it, how to obtain
participation of Christ.' The false doctrine of Transubstantiation
betokens 'the loss of the mystery of faith in the real participation
of Christ'.[93] The Puritans understood what a great Roman
Catholic layman of the twentieth century, Baron von Hügel,
called 'the mixed spirituality' of the Gospels. Jesus Himself hears
the voice at baptism, not as a result of spiritual experience alone,
but 'by physical contact with physical water'. The woman with
the issue of blood is made whole by her faith, 'but her faith aroused
on occasion of, and manifesting itself by physical contact' with,
the hem of our Lord's garment.[94] So Lewis Bayly compares the
Sacrament to other mighty works of Jesus: 'The Sacramental
bread and wine therefore are not bare signifying signes but such
as where-with Christ doth indeed exhibit and give to every worthy
Receiver not only his Divine virtue and efficacy, but also his very
Body and Blood, as verily he gave to his Disciples the Holy Ghost
by the sign of his sacred Breath; or health to the diseased by the
Word of his mouth, or touch of his hand or garment.'[95]

There is a kind of psycho-physical parallelism in some of the
Puritan explanations of the mystery of the Eucharist. 'These
outward symbolicall or sacramental actions serve to no other end,
but to signifie unto us these inward actions of the minde and will,
whereby we apprehend and receive Christ to our salvation.'[96]

[92] *Works*, p. 566.
[93] ibid., p. 563; cf. H. Smith, *Works*, pp. 57, 63; in the Anglican tradition the
famous words of R. Hooker, *Ecclesiastical Polity*, V.67; cf. C. Wesley, op. cit., No. 57:

> *Sure and real is the grace,*
> *The manner be unknown.*

[94] von Hügel, *Essays and Addresses*, II.78-81.
[95] *Practice of Piety*, pp. 252-3.
[96] William Perkins, *Workes*, II.83.

'When the faithful receive the bread and wine', says Henry Smith, 'one like to the Son of God seemeth to come unto them which fills them with peace and joy and grace that they marvel what it was that they received besides bread and wine';[97] and Bayly even goes so far as to say: 'In the same instant of time that the worthy receiver eateth with his mouth the Bread and Wine of the Lord he eateth also with the mouth of his Faith the very Body and Blood of Christ.'[98]

Faith and reverence are necessary to a right receiving. Richard Vines declares that 'many have an hundred times tasted bread and wine that never once tasted the body and blood of Christ'.[99] Later generations have labelled this 'Receptionism'. It is found in Richard Hooker.[100] Some such doctrine is a necessary safeguard against a mechanical and magical view of the Sacrament. But the Puritans had no doubt of a real presence of Christ in the Supper, and Samuel Rutherford could advertise a postponed Communion by saying that Christ would be all the more welcome when He came.[101]

(4) *The 'realism' of Puritanism sacramental teaching is qualified by the Reformed understanding of the 'eschatological distance' between Christ and us.*[102]

Christ is in heaven at the right hand of God; we are upon earth. The sacraments anticipate the Parousia; they do not precipitate it as the false doctrine of Transubstantiation would imply, thus overthrowing the very nature of a sacrament.

This transubstantiation, and consubstantiation is against the nature of a Sacrament in generall, against the analogy of our other Sacrament, or baptisme, against the most usual phrases in the Old Testament, against the humane nature of Christ, against his state of Glorification, and against the revealed will of God, which saith that Christ shall remaine in Heaven untill the day of judgment.[103]

---

[97] *Works*, I.51; cf. L. Bayly, *Practice of Piety*, p. 243; R. Vines, *Treatise of Lord's Supper*, p. 85.

[98] op. cit., pp. 251-2; cf. Charles Smyth's elucidation of Bucer, *Cranmer and the Reformation under Edward VI*, pp. 25 ff.

[99] op. cit., p. 252.

[100] *Ecclesiastical Polity*, V.57.

[101] *Letters*, XXXIII.112.

[102] The phrase 'eschatological distance' is based on Calvin and is borrowed from T. F. Torrance, *Kingdom and Church* (1956), p. 130.

[103] W. Ames, *Marrow of Divinity*, p. 184; cf. Article XXVIII, *Book of Common Prayer*.

The union between Christ and ourselves in the Sacrament is a real union, but it is a union of the Holy Spirit. As Walter Marshal puts it in words we have already quoted, and which correspond closely to a passage in Calvin:

Though Christ be in Heaven and we on Earth, yet he can join our Souls and Bodies to his at such a distance, without any substantial change of either, by the same infinite Spirit dwelling in him and us, and so our flesh will become his, when it is quickened by his Spirit, and his flesh ours as truly as if we did eat his flesh and drink his Blood, and he will be in us himself by his Spirit who is one with him, and who can unite us more closely to Christ than any material substance can do, or who can make a more close and intimate union betwixt Christ and us.[104]

Thus to the question 'But is not Christ's body present on earth, and in the sacrament?' Baxter has to reply:

We are sure he is in heaven, and we are sure that their doctrine is a fiction contrary to sense, reason and Scripture, that say the consecrated bread and wine are substantially turned into the very body and blood of Christ, and are no longer bread and wine. But how far the presence of Christ's soul and body extendeth is a question unfit for man's determination, unless we better knew what glorified souls and bodies are: we see that the sun is eminently in the heaven; and yet whether its lucid beams be a real part of its substance, which are here on earth, or how far they extend, we know not; nor know we how the sun differeth in greatness and glory, from the soul and body of Christ: nor know when an angel is in the room with us, and when not: these things are unfit for our enquiry and decision.[105]

Earlier, Henry Smith, who as we have seen does not regard the elements as bare signs, had applied to the Lord's Supper the words of the angel at the sepulchre, 'He is not here: he is risen', and had pertinently asked transubstantiationists why we are

---

[104] *Gospel Mystery*, p. 44; cf. Calvin, *Inst.*, 4.17.10, quoted Torrance, *Kingdom and Church*, p. 131: 'But though it seems an incredible thing that the flesh of Christ, while at such a distance from us in respect of space, should be food to us, let us remember how far the secret virtue of the Holy Spirit far surpasses all our conceptions and how foolish it is to wish to measure its immensity by our feeble capacity. Therefore what our mind does not comprehend let faith conceive, that the Spirit truly unites things separated by space.'

[105] *Works*, XIX.83, q.10.

summoned in the liturgy to lift up our hearts if Christ is all in our mouths.[106]

It may well be this which accounts for the apparent doctrine of the 'Real Absence' in Philip Doddridge's *The Rise and Progress of Religion in the Soul*—written in the next century. Just as Baxter is fearful of those who would rest in ordinances and not press on to the heavenly inheritance, so Doddridge looks beyond sacramental types and shadows to 'that nobler and more immediate worship where even these memorials shall be no longer necessary . . . but a living present Redeemer shall be the everlasting joy of those who here in his absence have delighted to commemorate his death'.[107] Joseph Stennett's lines express simply the important paradox of which the Puritans were so well aware— that there is a real spiritual union with Christ sealed and conveyed in the sacraments, but reaching its final consummation only in the Last Day:

> *We see Thee at Thy table, Lord*
> *By faith with great delight:*
> *Oh how refined those joys will be*
> *When faith is turned to sight.*[108]

SUMMARY AND CONCLUSION

We conclude therefore that Puritan sacramental devotion was based on regular and solemn observance of the Lord's command, an attempt to understand its meaning while not denying its mystery, and a fidelity to Scripture in interpreting it. The Puritans lived at a time when sacraments were remembered as 'the hinge of the priesthood's power, the very badge of the popish religion'.[109] Yet they did not repudiate what they accepted as the ordinances of Christ, or show themselves insensitive to the 'sacramental principle'. We do not find many Puritan passages of the sublimity of Richard Hooker's; yet we must not imagine that our authors are not moved to intense rapture by the sacramental theme. Owen becomes less of an Aristotle and more of a pastor in his sacramental discourses. Baxter, and later Watts, handle the holy things with intensity and power. These words of

---

[106] *Works*, p. 56; cf. Bayly, *Practice of Piety*, p. 244.
[107] cf. Baxter, *Works*, XXIII.189 ff.
[108] *Works*, IV, *Hymns for the Lord's Supper*, No. 12.
[109] The phrase is Nuttall's, p. 92.

Thomas Goodwin have more than a hint of St Bernard of Clair-vaux:

> Many things in a sermon thou understandest not, and haply not many sermons; or if thou doest, yet findest not thy portion in them; but here to be sure thou mayest. Of Sermons, some are for comfort, some to inform, some to excite; but here in the Sacrament is all thou canst expect. Christ is here light, and wisdom, and comfort and all to thee. He is here an eye to the blind, a foot to the lame; yea everything to every one.[110]

The privileges received through the Sacraments were a part of the privileges of the whole life of the Church. The Puritan way was not solitary. It is sometimes suggested that 'John Bunyan's Christian had to leave home and kindred and set out on a lonely path. Here and there a companion joined him, but his pilgrimage remained a terribly solitary affair till he got to its end beyond the river'.[111] This not only ignores the second part of *Pilgrim's Progress*; it does less than justice to Evangelist, Interpreter and the House Beautiful, to say nothing of the shepherds on the Delectable Mountains, and the most intimate fellow-pilgrims of Christian. The Puritans believed in the Communion of Saints, which included the earthly fellowship of God's people, as well as the whole company of heaven.[112] And they claimed for the small local company of believers an intimacy of fellowship and a Catholic status which is in accord with what P. T. Forsyth, Sir Edwyn Hoskyns and others in our own day have stated about the New Testament Church. As Thomas Goodwin puts it: 'A church, a particular church, the church of Corinth, is the body of Christ in particular, as well as the whole church is the body to him in general. . . . This church of Corinth therefore, was as truly a body to Jesus Christ and a whole body to him, as the church universal was the whole body, and had all the privileges of the body.'[113]

---

[110] *Works*, XI.408.
[111] H. Northcott, *The Venture of Prayer*, p. 44.
[112] e.g. Bolton's *Directions*, p. 26; Gouge, *Workes*, I.242; Baxter, *Works*, XXIII.302.
[113] *Works*, I.539; cf. Hoskyns and Davey, *The Riddle of the New Testament* (First published 1917, 1947 edn), p. 25; cf. also P. T. Forsyth, *Church and Sacraments*, pp. 65 ff.; A. M. Ramsey, *The Gospel and the Catholic Church* (1956 edn), p. 47, who quotes Forsyth.

Type of the wise, who soar, but never roam—
True to the kindred points of Heaven and Home

WILLIAM WORDSWORTH

Most people have forgotten nowadays what a home can mean though some of us have come to realize it as never before. It is a kingdom of its own in the midst of the world, a haven of refuge amid the turmoil of our age, nay more a sanctuary. It is not founded on the shifting sands of private and public life, but has its peace in God.

DIETRICH BONHOEFFER

CHAPTER FOUR

THE CHURCH IN THE HOUSE

THE Puritans regarded every household as a religious community. Perkins describes the family as 'a little church';[1] so does Gouge, who also calls it 'a seminary of the Church and commonwealth, a beehive in which is the stock'.[2] 'A Christian family', says Baxter, 'is a church . . . a society of Christians combined for the better worshipping and serving God.'[3]

The Puritans did not deny that there were advantages in the single life. It brought liberty in time of persecution, and freedom from the distractions of family concerns. But continency was deemed a particular gift of God, like health or wealth, not given to every one, and not to be enforced against His will. The monastic life whether coenobitic or solitary was deplored. Perkins says that voluntary poverty is against the Scripture, and a man must follow both his general calling of worship and love to his fellows, and his particular calling of service to the commonwealth in accorance with the second table of the law. A kind of monasticism may be necessary in apostolic missions or persecutions, but normally 'God's grace may be as well exercised in the family as in the cloister'. Neither can it be claimed that discipline and communion with God demand complete withdrawal from family life. The family is a 'Schoole of Christ', and there we can learn all the necessary virtues, and practice all needful spiritual exercises.[4]

The Puritans were scornful of those who seemed to regard virginity as a more excellent way than marriage, and yet regarded marriage as a Sacrament. They maintained that this set one supposed Sacrament (Orders) against another (Marriage).[5] Most of the Puritans did not think it appropriate to regard marriage as a Sacrament. Like Calvin, they exposed the false Vulgate rendering of '*mysterion*' in Ephesians 5[25] as '*Sacramentum*',

---

[1] *Workes*, p. 865.　　　[2] *Works*, II.10.　　　[3] *Works*, IV.75.
[4] W. Perkins, op. cit., pp. 703-4.　　　[5] W. Gouge, *Workes*, II.72.

and confined the title and solemnity of Sacraments to the two
institutions which are the signs of the Divine Covenant which
brought the Church into being. Lesser private convenants within
the Church have not their universal significance. Sacraments
proper should show forth the redeeming grace of God in its
entirety; other ceremonies for the hallowing of human relationships, or the investiture of Church officers, are subsidiary to
those.[6] The extreme Independents seem to have regarded the
marriage ceremony as a civil rather than a religious matter.[7]

There is much Puritan counsel about the choice of a wife and
the preparation for marriage. Henry Smith suggests five rules for
the former: Report (i.e. the lady's reputation), looks (does she
appear godly?), speech ('or rather her silence'!), apparel (i.e.
sobriety of dress), and company. Gouge thinks health and a
common religious faith very important too.[8] Puritans had
something of the Jewish and biblical attitude to betrothal, and
were strongly in favour of 'contracts' before marriage solemnized
in Church. We are able to overhear Richard Greenham exhorting
two of his young parishioners at such a ceremony on the duties
for which they must prepare. The husband is the head of the
wife, but the purpose of this is that he may further her salvation
and present her blameless before Christ; the wife is no passive
partner, for she may win the unbelieving husband, and much
more, assist in grace the faithful, while remembering that she is
'principally espoused unto Christ'.[9]

The Puritan attitude to the married relationship of husband
and wife was enlightened. Due benevolence in the sense of
1 Corinthians 7[4] is seen to be of necessity, but marriage must not
be legalized licence.[10] Though the husband is the head of the
wife, this does not mean that the woman is an inferior soul.[11]
Husband and wife should treat one another with loving dignity.
Sentimental endearments are deplored, but true affection should
be manifest. Above all there must be patience, and a readiness to
forgive even the sin of adultery.[12] False idealism is no help to

[6] Baxter, however, was not prepared to quibble about the number of the Sacraments. He distinguishes three senses in which the term may be used: *Works*, XIV.449 f.
[7] See Horton Davies, pp. 44-5.
[8] *Sermons*, pp. 20 ff; cf. Gouge, op. cit., pp. 104 ff, Baxter, *Works*, IV.22-5, who is
very concerned that lust is distinguished from love.
[9] *Workes*, pp. 154-5; cf. Baxter, *Works*, IV.116-75.
[10] cf. Gouge, *Workes*, II.130, Bolton, *Workes*, 242 f.
[11] Bolton, ibid., 245.
[12] Gouge, op. cit., p. 115.

marriage, for, as Bolton says, 'two Angells are not met together in a Matrimoniall state, but a sonne and daughter of Adam'.[13] There is not much difference between Puritan advice and that of St Francis of Sales, except that the latter with his sacramental view of marriage sees a significance in the marriage ring which the Puritans would repudiate.

Procreation is not the only purpose of marriage, and the union must not be broken for want of children. But children are the great blessing of marriage, and parents must watch over them by prayer, as well in the pre-natal period as afterwards. Bodily chastisement is an appropriate and Scriptural form of correction, provided it be adjusted to the psychology of the child, and applied in love and prayer and not to relieve parental feelings![14]

The household is viewed in its relation to Christ's mystical body and 'what the preacher is in the pulpit, the same the house-holder is in the house'.[15] He must direct the lives of all its members, and assemble them at least twice daily for family worship.[16] Model prayers for this are frequently provided to help those who would otherwise find its conduct difficult. Night offices are deplored as an ordinary rule, and Gouge scoffs at the canonical hours, grounded on superstition and legends of Christ's life. Says Baxter:

... this is but to serve God with irrational and hurtful ceremony that will not be drawn to a life of love and spiritual worship: unless men did irrationally place the service of God in praying this hour rather than another, they might see how improvidently and sinfully they lose their time in twice dressing and undressing and in the intervals of their sleep, when they might spare all that time by sitting up the longer or rising the earlier for the same employment. Besides what tendency it hath to the destruction of health by cold and interruption of necessary rest; when God approveth not of the disabling of the body or destroying our health, or shortening life (no more than of murder or cruelty to others); but only calleth us to deny our unnecessary sensual delights, and use the body so as it may be most serviceable to the soul and to him.'[17]

---

[13] op. cit., p. 241.
[14] Gouge, *Workes*, II.106, who quotes Augustine; also ibid., pp. 386 ff, 'Pattern Prayers for Husbands and Wives, etc.'.
[15] L. Bayly, *Practice of Piety*, p. 158n., cited, without references, from Augustine.
[16] Baxter, *Works*, IV.48 ff; cf. Horton Davies, App. D, p. 278.
[17] *Works*, IV.239.

Presumably Puritans would hardly have appreciated Bernard of Clairvaux's bidding his monks remember in their vigils the prevenience of Him whose love anticipates their night watches.[18] In any case the life of a household cannot be organized quite as a monastery.

Or can it? It is impossible to read the Puritan directions about household religion without recalling the family at Little Gidding. One of the differences between the Ferrar and the Puritan rules was in the matter of night watches, which the Ferrars, after long consideration, began to keep, though on a voluntary basis. They kept sentinel to watch for the second coming of the Lord Jesus, but William Gouge, while recognizing that at times, as the Scripture evidences, this may be legitimate, interprets the Lord's command as concerned with spiritual alertness.[19] The Ferrars also were more liturgical in their devotions and hourly weekday offices, and no doubt in consequence less verbose. But not even Nicholas Ferrar's latest biographer can make him a Tractarian before time. He describes the Ferrar piety as 'biblical rather than sacramental', and makes clear that Little Gidding was not intended as a revival of monasticism.[20] He quotes Hacket to the effect that the Ferrar family covenanted between themselves, 'to live in as strict a way, according to the Gospel of Christ, as good rules could chalk out and human infirmity undergo'.[21] Nicholas's own quoted comment on the Lord's Day is thoroughly Puritan; it is to be 'a day of rest not of pleasures; it frees us from bodily labours, but it should the more intend the exercises of the mind. God blessed the day and sanctified it; they must go together. If we would have it happy we must make it holy.'[22]

[18] Sermon LXIX, *Cantica Canticorum* (trans. S. J. Eales, 1895), pp. 425-6. Mentioned without reference by von Hügel, *Essays and Addresses*, II.225.

[19] See A. L. Maycock, *Nicholas Ferrar*, pp. 216 ff.

[20] ibid., p. 220. The implied antithesis between biblical and sacramental piety is perhaps a little unfortunate. The fact remains that at a time when separatists were insisting on weekly communion, the Ferrars attended celebrations once a month, and at the Great Festivals. In his edition of the Ferrar papers (Cambridge, 1938, pp. 5, 185) B. Blackstone suggests that on his continental travels Nicholas Ferrar would be influenced by the devotions of the oratories of St Philip Neri, but the evidence he brings forward for this is most unconvincing. For Nicholas Ferrar's hatred of the Mass, see Blackstone, p. 75.

[21] A. L. Maycock, op. cit., p. 198.

[22] ibid., p. 208. The household of Sir Thomas More, Catholic though he was, is of the pattern to which the Puritans later tried to conform. This makes the following comment on Roper's account of More's rule of piety most unfortunate. 'Reading passages of this description we come to understand that Luther and Tyndale and

THE LORD'S DAY

At the beginning of the English Reformation, Sabbatarianism was a Catholic rather than a Protestant characteristic. William Tyndale wrote thus, in answer to Sir Thomas More: 'And as for the Sabboth a great matter, we be lords over the Sabboth; and may yet change it into the Monday or any other day as we see need, or may make every tenth day holy day only if we see a cause why. We may make two every week if it were expedient, and one not enough to teach the people. Neither were there any cause to change it from the Saturday than to put difference between us and the Jews, and lest we should become servants unto the day, after their superstition.'[23] Calvin, too, was much more liberal in his interpretation of the Fourth Commandment than the Puritans.[24] For Protestant Sabbatarianism we must go to Luther's contemporary Carlstadt—though his doctrine of the Sabbath, while legalistic, was also quietist—and to Martin Bucer.[25] It is Bucer's 'programme for England', in his *De Regno Christi* (1550), which insists upon the necessity of Sabbath observance enforced by Royal Command, and anticipates Puritan teaching. For them the discipline of a strict Sunday—with the addition of occasional fasts and weekday lectures—replaced the multitude of Catholic Holy Days. It was God's day that was kept, so the Puritans believed, and not a festival in honour of mere man, however worthy. Our whole redemption was commemorated each Sabbath, and not some fragment, which, isolated, might obscure the vastness of God's grand design. Moreover, if the Puritans took seriously the command to keep holy one day of the week,

those that followed them destroyed, or wanted to destroy, the technique of the most difficult of all arts—the art of human sanctity—and that as revealed by divine inspiration, and shown forth in saintly practice within the Church throughout the fifteen hundred years that separated our Lord's earthly life from theirs' (W. E. Campbell, *Erasmus, Tyndal and More* (1949), p. 145).

[23] *Works*, III.97-8.

[24] *Inst.*, II.viii.28 ff.

[25] The Carlstadt tract is *'Von dem Sabbat und gebotten feyertagen, Andres Carolstat, MDXXIIII Jena'*. 'Do you ask what is anybody to do for such a long time on Sabbath for sheer boredom? Answer: a man ought to . . . do nothing and just suffer . . . for his boredom and passing of time is a kind of spiritual circumcision and preparation for receiving God's work; . . . it would be well for a man if he sat all Sunday with his head in his hands and bewailed his sins. . . .' Quoted H. Gerdes, *Luthers Streit mit den Schwarmern* (Gottingen, 1955), p. 31. I owe this reference to Professor E. Gordon Rupp. For Bucer see *Martini Bucer, Opera Latina*, ed. Wendel, Vol. XV, *De Regno Christi Libri Duo 1550* (Paris, 1955), pp. 114 f., 81 f. There is a parallel page edition of the 1558 French translation (Paris 1954).

F

they regarded work on the other six days as equally of divine injunction. Though they would encourage gatherings of the faithful for weekday worship, and diurnal household and private devotions, they hint at the danger that too many days of obligation would encroach upon the just claims of men's divinely ordained callings in the world.

Richard Greenham declares: 'Our Easter Day, our Ascension Day, our Whitsuntide is every Lord's Day.'[26] This, he says, is the appropriate day for any special thanksgiving. 'For as the Jews used the Sabboth as a day to remember with thanksgiving their creation; so may we use that day for a thankeful remembrance of our redemption, because in it we may meditate of all those benefits which our Saviour Christ by his nativitie, circumcision, passion, resurrection and ascension hath purchased for us.' It is ridiculous to deem every day a Sabbath, 'as though we should confound and shuffle together our working days and resting days'. We should give a tithe of all our time to God, and where convenient 'it were nothing but equal' that we should meet twice every weekday in public worship. But 'the worship of God must, in the six daies be used at such seasons as in wisedom are so separated and divided to that ende without any hinderance of our lawfull and necessarie callings, as it doth not take up the principall but shreds and overplus of our vocation'.

It is interesting to find that Lewis Bayly gives that place to the keeping of the Lord's Day, as the guarantee of order, which the modern Anglo-Catholic would ascribe to the episcopate. The commandment to keep holy the Sabbath, he says, was in the midst of Moses' tables of stone, and this signifies that 'the keeping of it is the best help to the keeping of all the rest. . . . The mother of all religion and good discipline is the Church. Take away the Sabbath and let every man serve God when he listeth and what will shortly become of Religion, and that peace and order which God will have to be kept in his Church?'[27] Just as Catholics often suggest that Christ instructed His disciples in those details of Church order not specifically mentioned in Scripture, during the forty days between Easter and the Ascension, so Bayly claims this convenient lacuna to be the time of the

---

[26] All citations from R. Greenham, 'A Treatise of the Sabboth', *Workes*, pp. 159 ff cf. John Dod, *The Ten Commandments*, pp. 117 ff.

[27] *Practice of Piety*, p. 185.

Lord's institution of the Christian Sabbath on the first day of the week. [28]

We may charge Greenham more than Bayly with giving undue weight to Old Testament precept, and saying comparatively little about the Day of Resurrection. Greenham says that the Sabbath was changed by the Apostles, 'not as private men, but as men guided by the spirit of God', for several reasons. The first is 'for the avoyding of superstition, wherewith the Iewes had infected it'. This would doubtless seem particularly relevant just after the Reformation. Then Greenham mentions the great events which establish the pre-eminence of the first day of the week—it was the day of Christ's Resurrection, of the beginning of Creation, and of the giving of the Holy Ghost. Like most of the Puritans, Greenham seems anxious to establish the Sabbath as a truth of Natural Theology. He does not, for instance, dwell on the Deuteronomic version of the Fourth Commandment, which by its stress on redemption and on mercy should appeal to Christians: 'Thou shalt remember that thou wast a slave in the land of Egypt, and the Lord thy God brought thee out thence by a mighty hand and by a stretched out arm; therefore the Lord thy God commanded thee to keep holy the Sabbath day.' Exodus 20[11] is Greenham's proof text, because he wishes to demonstrate that the obligation is incumbent upon all men; it is no mere Jewish law, given 'for the hardness of men's hearts'. 'That which was needefull to continue Adam in his innocencie is also needefull to recover us and to continue us in our recovery.'

Thus the Sabbath is no type and shadow which has ending ('there were no figures until sin came into the world from which our parents were yet free'); it is no mere ceremonial law abrogated with the end of Judaism, a sign of the pre-Christian divorce between God and man, and the separation between Jew and Gentile. It is a law written by the finger of God, not merely by Moses. It is a moral law (like matrimony, says Bayly) which, according to Greenham, we must keep 'in truth though in weakness, knowing that the rigour of the law being gone with the curse and ceremonie, we have a promise to have our weakness and defects herein forgiven us in Christ as we have in all other things'.

---

[28] Acts 1[3]. See Bayly, op. cit., p. 175. He also agrees that during that time 'Christ appointed what ministers should teach, and how they should govern his Church to the world's end'.

It is very difficult to find any evidence in Puritan writings for
F. W. Dillistone's statement of the Puritan attitude. He declares
that for Puritanism

> *all* time is evil, except the one sacred day of each week, which has
> been given by God as the token of what the life of the elect will be in
> heaven. In this conception, which is obviously derived from the strict
> Sabbatarianism of post-exilic Judaism, the six days are especially
> associated with labour and travail and the curse of earthly existence,
> the seventh with rest and holiness and the bliss of heavenly existence. . . .
> Traditionally, this one day in seven has had as its central activity the
> declaring of the law of God and the renewal of the submission of the
> elect to its commands and ordinances. Special days such as Christmas
> and Good Friday have no essential part to play in this view of time; . . .
> the celebration of the Lord's Supper has no essential place. . . .[29]

Here is the analytic and philosophic theologian writing without
any reference to actual Church History! So far from time in
itself being regarded as evil, the Puritans took the Augustinian
view that the world was created *with* time, and that therefore
Adam in his innocence needed to keep the Sabbath in order that
his heart might not be so enraptured with the delights of nature
as to be withdrawn from the praise of God. The Puritans believed
that they served God in their ordinary callings, but they were too
good Sacramentalists to regard all days alike.

> There is as much difference betweene the Sabbath and other days as
> betweene the consecrated bread we receive at the Lord's Table and the
> common bread that we receive at our own table. This is true, that every
> one must serve God on the sixe days and all our life long, yet so as he
> may and must do the duties of his special calling withal. But on the
> seventh day, we must not only serve God, but we must serve him in
> the duties of religion and mercie only. As for example: God's children
> will not eate meate at their own table without craving God's blessing
> upon it: but when we are to come to the table of the Lorde they use a
> greater and more solemn preparation, because they expect a greater
> and more excellent blessing.[30]

Richard Baxter is less interested in Exodus, and speaks of the
Lord's Day rather than the Sabbath, though he regards the name

---

[29] *Christianity and Symbolism* (1955), p. 91.
[30] J. Dod, *The Ten Commandments*, p. 124.

as 'not worth contending about'.[31] He is also aware of that Pharisaism, which, even among Christians, profanes the day. 'Take heed of the hypocritical and censorious temper which turneth the holy observation into a ceremonious abstinence from lawful things.'[32] But the Puritans use a common figure of speech to explain just why, apart from the worship of God, the Sabbath is to be observed. It is, says Greenham, 'the schoole day, the faire day, the market day, the feeding day of the soul', and again, 'an holy schoole to teach us the worship of God'.[33] So Baxter, when he counsels the faithful of Kidderminster to equip themselves by reading, suggests that time for this must be found even by the hardest worked, and that the Lord's day should be spent 'wholly in such things'.[34] Puritan piety was to be informed and in the widest sense intellectual, and the Sabbath served this end. The day was not to be spent in idleness; it was not a day of human rest, but the Lord's. No mere waiting upon appointed ceremonies was enough; there must be understanding, and this could not be deepened without the discipline of a day set apart. And yet the activities of the Lord's Day were considered the sublimest re-creation: 'Is it not a recreation for a Christian to heare the voice of Christ, and for a sheep of Christ to feed in his pasture? Is it not a recreation for a person condemned to come where he may get his pardon sealed to him? and his sicke soule to be healed? Is it not a recreation for a man subject to death to heare a direction that will lead him to life?'[35]

PUBLIC WORSHIP

And so the Lord's day with its union of public and private worship was the grand climax of Puritan household religion. Lewis Bayly describes its right ordering.[36] It must be prepared for on Saturday night, and there must be no indulgence of the flesh in the preceding hours. Family devotions will be a little more brief on Sunday morning to allow for an especial private preparation for worship and the assembling of the household in

[31] *Works*, IV.240.
[32] ibid., 247-8.
[33] *Workes*, p. 159; cf. Bayly, *Practice of Piety*, p. 185; Dod, op. cit., p. 128; Geree, *Character of an Old English Puritane*, p. 3.
[34] *Works*, XXII.4-5.
[35] J. Dod, *The Ten Commandments*, p. 136.
[36] op. cit., 211 ff; cf. *A Garden of Spirituall Flowers*.

church. The walk to church will be accompanied by silent meditations on suitable Scriptures, but once the sanctuary is gained, all private thoughts must be laid aside, and the whole heart and mind given over to joining in the service in 'the manner of the Church wherein thou livest'. Bayly has good counsel to offer if the preacher be too cumbersome, but it will be well for every member of the household to listen intently, and to look at the preacher closely, for after dinner, there will be an examination. Those in the family who remember the sermon and understand it will be commended, but the head of the house must not discourage those 'whose memories or capacities are weaker'.[37] He will 'rub over' the main lessons of the Exposition and, after a psalm, go on to catechize, provided that all is over in time for afternoon Church. Dinner will be shared, either by having a few poor Christians in, or sending food 'to the poor who lie sick in the back lane'. The final act of the day for the head of the house, before his private prayers and meditation *en famille*, will be the visiting of sick neighbours and the attempt to reconcile those at variance. In Bayly's concluding devotions there is no pretence of having kept the Sabbath perfectly, or suggestion that its dutiful observance can be offered as a meritorious work to God. The saint can only confess: 'I know that thou art a consuming fire, I acknowledge that I am but withered stubble. . . . I have nothing to present unto thee for a satisfaction, but onely those bloody wounds, bitter Death and Passion which thy blessed sonne my only Saviour hath suffered for me.'

From this, we can substantiate some of the characteristics of Puritan worship of which Dr Horton Davies has written. It was above all to be worship of the congregation, and therefore in the mother tongue and in contemporary language. There is no doubt that in the early years after the Reformation this brought a vividness to public worship which could offset the drab austerity of its externals. William Perkins devotes all his patristic learning to prove that worship in the vernacular was customary in the first centuries, and adduces Tertullian, Jerome and Origen in support.[38] We find Puritans anticipating objections of 'Modern Churchmen' to the Prayer Book. In 1661 the Presbyterian ministers presented

---

[37] cf. W. Gouge, *Workes*, p. 303, who insists on constant catechism but which must not be allowed to be tedious, 'precept upon precept, line upon line'.

[38] *Workes*, II.557 ff.

their 'Exceptions against the *Book of Common Prayer*' to the Bishops. They quarrelled with archaisms in the collects and services, such as 'with my body I thee *worship*' and 'Till death us *depart*', in the Marriage Order, and they demanded a new royal translation of the Scriptures although the Authorized Version was only half a century old![39]

The centre of public worship was the sermon, the 'opening' of the Scriptures. This was never considered as the mere 'braying' of men, but as the living proclamation of God's word. Greenham says that our hands are best employed when they are receiving the Sacrament, our eyes when they are reading, our feet when they bring us to the house of God, and our ears when we hear God's word. Hearing the word is Mary's good part which shall not be taken away. So we must be prepared for hearing and 'we must heare the word as good Catholickes, that is, we must not heare the worde by parcels and by clauses as we list, and give our eare untill it come to our especiall sinne, and sit quietly till our boyle be touched: but wee must heare universally as well the things that mislike us, as the things that please us'. We must also hear continually and 'bring a desire to practise the things we hear. . . . If in hearing the word I draw not neere to the mercie of God I shall draw neere to his wrath, if not to my salvation, sure to my destruction.'[40] The word of the minister is the word of the Lord, because of Christ's commission, 'whoso heareth you heareth me'. Bayly declares that to hear as did those who walked with Christ to Emmaus 'is the surest note of Christ's saints; the truest mark of Christ's sheep; the apparantest sign of God's Elect; the very blood as it were which uniteth us to be the spiritual kindred, brethren and sisters of the son of God'.[41]

[39] Horton Davies, pp. 146-152.
[40] *Workes*, pp. 332-5.
[41] L. Bayly, *Practice of Piety*, pp. 214-15; cf. Baxter's *Directions for Hearing*, *Works*, IV.251 ff.

God gives daily bread to all men even the wicked without our prayer; but we pray in this prayer that we may recognise this goodness of God, and with gratitude receive our daily bread.

MARTIN LUTHER

This instant now may I receive
The answer of His powerful prayer;
This instant now by Him I live,
His prevalence with God declare,
And soon my spirit in His hands,
Shall stand where my Forerunner stands.

CHARLES WESLEY

CHAPTER FIVE

THE PRAYER OF FAITH

THE Puritans had no doubt that the public ordinances of the Christian faith were indispensable, and Richard Greenham, in an aside, assumes as axiomatic that there is a greater blessing 'to bee due by the Lord his owne promise'[1] to public devotion than to private. But John Preston and Richard Baxter are perhaps more conscious that it is superficially easier to join in public than in private discipline. The former writes of prayer: 'Though you perform it in your families and meet in the congregation you must not think that this is enough, you are bound to a private performance of this duty';[2] and Baxter goes farther when he says: 'We are fled so far from the solitude of superstition, that we have cast off the solitude of contemplative devotion. . . . We seldom read of God's appearing by himself or his angels to any of his prophets or saints in a throng, but frequently when they are alone.'[3] Robert Bolton agrees with this emphasis on the value of private prayer, and goes so far as to say that spiritual joy in contrast with carnal is 'ordinarily most free, full, and at the highest in solitarinesse, soliloquies and the most retired exercises of the soul'.[4]

Although private prayer is intimate and solitary, it does not follow that a man needs no instruction in these most inward duties and outpourings of his soul. True, as John Preston says, 'there never was a man in any extreme want but he knew how to express himself',[5] and Bunyan in his less academic, brusquer way, maintains that prayer is simply 'a groaning out of our condition before the Lord'.[6] Even so, we must have some understanding of what prayer according to the Spirit is; we must be

---

[1] *Workes*, p. 167.
[2] *The Saint's Daily Exercise*, p. 84.
[3] *Works*, XXIII.333-4. He refers to similar sentiments in Chrysostom and Cyprian.
[4] *Workes*, p. 60.
[5] op. cit., p. 83.
[6] *A Discourse Touching Prayer, Works*, I.623 ff, esp. pp. 631-4

warned of false methods, and exhorted to a discipline of devotion; for whereas animals and birds make noises when they want their food, we too often snatch at blessings without any recognition of God's Providence, and make any excuse to avoid our prayers. 'Oh! the starting-holes that the heart hath in time of prayer; none knows how many bye-ways the heart hath and back lanes to slip away from the presence of God.'[7]

Therefore the devotions of each day must be planned. The example of Daniel is frequently cited. 'He kneeled upon his knees three times a day and prayed and gave thanks before his God.'[8] Robert Bolton is said by his biographer to have prayed 'sixe times a day, twice by himself in private, twice in publique with his family, and twice with his wife'.[9] Morning and evening are the chief occasions for private prayer, even as they were the times of sacrifice in the Jewish Temple.[10] But besides this we must so cultivate communion with God as to be able to pray in season and out of season. 'Unto which prayers there is not required that we should use our voice or gestures of the body which are used in set prayers, . . . but sudden and short ejaculation, . . . a darting unto the Throne of Grace.'[11] This links the Puritans with the long tradition of Eastern and Western ejaculatory prayer, with the difference that they do not use it as a prelude to mystical experience.

THE WORDS OF PRAYER

There is however a practical problem which has always exercised, and to some extent divided, Protestant Christians. Can the soul hope to ascend to heaven on another man's words? Must not real prayer, inspired by the Holy Spirit, be extempore?

Dr Nuttall has reviewed some of the great controversies among Puritans on this score, and has shown that by the time of the Civil Wars, certain Puritans, 'acutely conscious of the working of the Holy Spirit, immediately, in their hearts, increasingly felt

[7] *A Discourse Touching Prayer, Works*, I.631.

[8] Daniel 6[10].

[9] E. B. Esq., *The Life and Death*, p. 24.

[10] cf. Lancelot Andrewes, *Preces Privatae*.

[11] J. Downame, *Guide to Godliness*, p. 210; cf. Baxter, *Works*, XXIII.315; W. Ames, *Marrow of Divinity*, p. 248; Bede Frost, *The Art of Mental Prayer*, p. 148; W. O. Chadwick, *John Cassian*; Francis of Sales, *Introduction*, pp. 77 ff; H. A. Hodges, *Introduction* p. 21 to E. Kadloubovsky, *Unseen Warfare* (1952).

there to be no place in worship for liturgies or read prayers'.[12]
Baxter and Owen differed here, the latter being vehemently
'against all Liturgies'.[13] But the Puritan Pastor seems to have
realized the necessity of teaching his people to pray in private, and
for this models were useful, as Owen agreed.[14] William Gouge
went so far as to say: 'Those who simply and altogether condemn
prescribed prayer doe thinke too childishly of God, and deal too
injuriously with God's little ones.'[15] The authors of guides to
godliness give much instruction here. A Puritan Bishop such as
Lewis Bayly counsels the use in private devotion of the Psalms as
appointed in the Prayer Book, and provides several alternative
pattern prayers for morning, evening, the Sacrament, and other
seasons. He does not, apparently, approve of the collect as the
proper form for private prayer. 'A prayer in private devotion
should be one continued speech rather than many broken
fragments.' And the Christian should be so familiar with Scriptural phrases that he can speak to God 'as well in his (God's)
own holy words' as in his native tongue.[16]

John Bunyan, on the other hand, declares that the Prayer
Book is virtually forbidden in Scripture by all the prohibitions
of feasts and new moons and vain repetitions. Even the Lord's
Prayer can become blasphemy if uttered without Spirit or understanding. Effectual praying is by the Spirit who convinces us
of sin, and in spite of this encourages us to go to God. The
Spirit alone cries: 'Father!' It is of little avail to have learnt
the Lord's Prayer and the Creeds if we have no knowledge of our
natural misery or of what it is to be brought to God through
Christ. The Lord's Prayer was never intended as a 'stinted form',
but as a model of prayer, a set of rules for praying. Those who
recite it blithely should be challenged as to their knowledge of the
clauses and the sincerity of their petitions.

Thus Bunyan contends, in words which have not lost their
timeliness, for the prayer which cries 'Abba, Father' from a
prodigal heart, and which does not presume on a paternal
benevolence which accepts the right password and requires

---

[12] Nuttall, p. 66.

[13] Owen's MS. *Twelve Arguments against Conformity*, was answered by Baxter's
Catholic Communion Defended, p. 26.

[14] e.g. *Works*, IV.347.

[15] *Workes*, I.211.

[16] Both quotations from *Practice of Piety*, p. 124.

nothing more. Earlier, John Preston had not gone so deep, but he had noted the obvious facts that set forms have been used as helps to prayer throughout the Church's history, and that a tie of words is not necessarily a tie of the Spirit. Perkins likewise believed that the spirit of grace and prayer in 'the party reading and the hearers' was what mattered, and that this need not be lacking in set forms.[17] The emphasis, however, is always on the principle that words and forms should be our guide and not our chain. All writers would agree that the Scriptures provide the pattern of personal prayer, not merely in language, but in their spirit of utter, childlike dependence upon God, and that the great danger of forms is that they may be used without regard to the sense 'while the tongue is a stranger to the heart, and speaketh not according to its desires'.[18] There were no Paters and Aves in Puritanism.

SOME FURTHER PROBLEMS OF PRAYER

William Gouge defines prayer as 'A right opening of the desire of the heart to God'.[19] This definition can in fact include the two kinds of prayer which in our chapter headings we have classified as the prayer of faith and the prayer of love—a distinction which roughly corresponds to that of Heiler's between prophetic (or faith) piety and mystical prayer. The prayer which is essentially petition, whether it be 'God be merciful to me a sinner', or 'Give us this day our daily bread', raises certain problems of which the Puritans were as well aware as any modern questioners. There is for instance, the inveterate poser which both Aquinas and Calvin consider: 'Why pray if God knows our wants already?'[20] William

---

[17] J. Preston, *Saint's Daily Exercise*, p. 82; W. Perkins, *The Lord's Prayer, Workes*, I.326 ff (wrongly given as 328)—and so for all citations. cf. J. Dod, who claims that 'Separatists and Schismatics' in their refusal to allow any forms of prayer are reproved by the Lord's Prayer, and the prescribed forms of the Old Testament (*A Plaine and Familiar Exposition of the Lord's Prayer*, p. 6).

[18] Baxter, *Works*, IV.285. In the next century, Isaac Watts, *Guide to Prayer*, judiciously mediates in the controversy.

[19] *Workes*, I.167.

[20] Aquinas, *Summa Theol.*, Part II (II), Q. 83, Art. 2 (a) (b): 'We need to pray to God not in order to make known to him our needs or desires but that we ourselves may be reminded of the necessity of having recourse to God in these matters . . . not that we may change the divine disposition, but that by our prayers we may obtain what God has appointed'; cf. Calvin, *Inst.* III.20.3: 'It was not so much for his (God's) sake as for ours.'

Perkins has a four-fold answer to this. We pray to show our submission and obedience, to show our true repentance, to show that we acknowledge God as the Giver of all things, and 'to ease our minds by praying out our hearts'. Preston and Gouge go a little farther. God indeed knows our wants, but do we? 'He will have thee know them. . . . For since he knows your wants he will be more ready to hear your requests.'[21] Prayer is worship; it is the condition of God's bestowing of His benefits, the acknowledgement of His attributes. It is not God who is changed by our prayers, but we ourselves. 'When you thinke you draw God to you with your arguments in truth you draw yourselves nearer to him.'[22] The less sophisticated Bunyan would have had an even simpler answer to the problem had he specifically raised it. Prayer is for him a groaning out of our condition; hence it is the natural cry of the soul. Truly God knows our every need, but the sincere Christian 'hath his prayers forced out of him by the anguish of his soul'.[23]

The Calvinist Perkins is also worried by a question which Calvin himself does not raise—Why must we pray, since God has already decreed what will come to pass? The answer is that God has ordained not only ends but means, and prayer is His appointed means of carrying out His decree.

The Puritans follow Luther and Calvin in commenting upon the Lord's Prayer at length.[24] The crux of the interpretation is 'Give us this day our daily bread', and writers are unanimous in referring this to the supplying of physical needs. Perkins deplores 'the vaine and frivolous' contention of Erasmus that earthly bread is not referred to. 'It is God's will that we should not cast the care of heavenly things only, but all our care upon him.' The petition also limits our demands to sufficient but not exorbitant supplies, and the very fact of our having to ask even for a piece of bread means that all is of grace, all depends on God. 'If we cannot merit

---

[21] J. Preston, *Saint's Daily Exercise*, p. 41; cf. W. Gouge, *Workes*, I.168 f, and W. Ames, *Marrow of Divinity*, p. 246, who says that we pray not to inform God of our desires, nor to change his will, 'but that we may . . . obtaine that of him which we believe he is willing to'.

[22] J. Preston, op. cit., p. 45.

[23] *A Discourse Touching Prayer*, *Works*, I.633.

[24] e.g. J. Dod, *A Plaine and Familiar Exposition of the Lord's Prayer;* William Gouge, *A Guide to goe to God; or an explanation of the Lord's Prayer;* and Baxter, *Works*, XIX. 121-58.

a piece of bread, what madness is it to think we can merit life everlasting?'[25]

John Preston realizes that the natural man, careless of God and the observance of religion, may have blessings thrust upon him which to the saints are denied. But the natural man's tenure of these blessings is temporary and uncertain. He may have them through his own aggression, and if so he has them with a curse. Like Ahab's possession of Naboth's vineyard or Gehazi's of Naaman's reward 'death goeth with them'. On the other hand, divine providence for a particular purpose of judgement or salvation may bestow blessings on wicked men, 'treasures of darkness', wisdom, kingdoms, crowns. But these are given only for the Church's sake, and, in the end, those who receive them will be smitten. Only the blessings received through prayer (through love, that is) are sure and certain.

The Puritans are also occupied with the problems of unanswered prayer. They urge the faithful to try their hearts, lest perchance, when the heavens are silent, they have asked anything amiss. It is so easy for our hearts to be deceived into petitioning for the satisfaction of our lusts. It is not that God regards our merits in answering; good works do not purchase benefits, and none of us can open a deposit account in the Kingdom of Heaven. As Bunyan says, pressing the details of the parable of the importunate man (for he knew not Jülicher), though God will not rise because we are His friends, He will because of our restless desires. And again, 'He loves to keep his people praying, and to find them ever knocking at the gate of heaven'. In all this we should remember that 'the Lord hath waited longer upon me, than I have waited upon him'.

Certain stock examples are used to illustrate from Scripture ways in which prayers have been answered differently from the petitioner's expectation. Paul arrived at Rome, but a prisoner; Naaman was cleansed, but for his humbling, in despised Jordan. The Lord will not be defeated because some military or political expedient to which we have joined our prayers is doomed. His

[25] The meaning of 'Epiousion', the word translated 'daily' is notoriously difficult: see e.g. A. H. McNeile's *Commentary on Matthew*, p. 79. More mystical writers such as St Teresa refer it to the bread of the Eucharist and so unlike the Puritans remove the petition from the common material realm. Some modern exegetes consider this an eschatological petition: 'Give us today a foretaste of the consummated kingdom where we shall eat bread with thee.' It is significant to compare the Puritan interpretation with that of Luther as summarized in Philip S. Watson, *Let God be God*, pp. 39-41.

cause is not lost when earthly arms are vanquished. 'The Lord
will help the Church after another manner that we dream not of.'
Let us leave it then to Him, for He is skilful and we can wait His
leisure. In the end, all frustrations will be overcome and all dis-
cords united in the triumph song of heaven. Thus the prayer of
the Christian will always be the prayer of Gethsemane and of the
Pater Noster—'Thy will be done'.[26]

Thomas Goodwin has a treatise on *The Return of Prayers*.[27] 'There
may be some prayers which you must be content never yourselves
to see answered in this world.'[28] And these may be prayers for
the Church. But God never refuses to answer His faithful servants
without great compensations—an increase of faith in them, an
assurance of His love (as to Moses), a David for a Saul, or a
quietness of heart (as to Hannah and Paul).[29] Sometimes indeed
we fail to notice answers to prayer and talk of second causes, or a
common providence.[30] We must learn to look for God's guiding
hand in the events of our lives, and we must persist in prayer in
spite of discouragements, for thus shall we be brought nearer to
God. John Owen declares that 'we can have no more faith that
our prayers are heard than we have faith that our persons are
accepted'. We may well be disappointed if we have not mortified
our lusts, or if we have neglected to treasure up former experiences
of God's hearing prayer.[31]

THE PRAYER OF CONFESSION

'The heart must be broken and humbled before the Lord will
own it as his, take up his abode with it, and rule in it.'[32] Thus
Thomas Hooker expresses the need for contrition and humiliation
which bring the sinner to confession. But these arise out of
adoration, and of the consciousness of the infinite gulf between
God and man. 'Nothing', says Owen, in his *Sacramental Discourses*,
so much 'brings God and man together as a due sense of our
infinite distance.'[33] The first waking thought must be of Him, and
the remembrance of His majesty begins each prayer. Thus the
meanness of our nature is revealed, and our desert of punishment.

---

[26] J. Preston, *Saint's Daily Exercise*, pp. 56-9; cf. W. Gouge, *Workes*, I.174.
[27] *Works*, III.359 ff.   [28] ibid., p. 365.   [29] ibid., pp. 366-76.
[30] ibid., p. 383.   [31] *Works*, IX.380.
[32] T. Hooker, *Application of Redemption*, Book IX.5.   [33] *Works*, IX.551.

Confession is the prayer which the Spirit most of all inspires, for His are the groanings we cannot utter. Richard Sibbes, in *The Bruised Reed*, discusses the necessity of being bruised: 'We must conceive of bruising either as a state into which God bringeth us, or as a duty to be performed by us.'[34] Henry Smith prays: 'Teach us to remember our sins that thou mayest forget them, and let our sorrow here prevent the sorrow to come.'[35] It is not merely the unregenerate man who groans in the consciousness of sin; no one was more aware than the Puritan of the problem of sin in believers. The redeemed soul is on pilgrimage through this world, and must find many places of repentance. Conversion is not an end of struggling, as Bunyan knew. The confession prescribed by Lewis Bayly for evening prayer is more passionate than that with which the day begins, for has there not been yet one more span of conscious life with its failures and yieldings and sins? The petitioner begs 'that my sins and uncleanness may be so bathed in (Christ's) blood, buried in his death, and hid in his wounds that they may never be more seen to shame me in this life, or to condemn me before thy judgement seat in the world which is to come. If it be thy blessed pleasure to adde more dayes unto my life, oh Lord adde more amendment unto my dayes'.[36]

A prerequisite of genuine confession is rigorous self-examination. The Puritan's life was to be above all else the scrutinized one. '*All is, if I have grace to use it so, as ever in my great Task-Master's eye.*'[37] Every duty is to be performed, every thought surveyed, as 'unto the Lord'. So Bayly gives counsel for the daily walk, its words and actions, and says that the day's events must be recalled in solitude before prayer. The Christian is advised: 'Labour daily more and more to see thine own misery through unbelief, self love and wilful breaches of God's law; and the necessity of God's mercy, through the merits of Christ's Passion, to be such; that if thou wert demanded, what is the vilest creature upon earth? thy conscience may answer mine own self, by reason of my great sins; and that if on the other side thou wert asked, what thou esteemest to be the most precious thing in the world? thy heart might answer, one drop of Christ's blood to wash away my sins. And as thou tenderest the salvation of thy soul, live not

---

[34] *Works*, I.47.   [35] *Works*, II.462.   [36] *Practice of Piety*, pp. 149-51.
[37] John Milton, *On His Being Arrived at the Age of Twenty-three.*

in any wilful filthiness: For true faith, and the purpose of sinning can never stand together.'[38]

We can see from this that the contrite Puritan was not for ever stirring up the cesspool of his iniquities. The intensely religious soul may be in danger of this, as were some of the Desert Fathers, but Dr Chadwick is able to quote some words of Richard Baxter as a corrective to one aspect of the spirituality of John Cassian: 'I was once wont to meditate on my own heart, and to dwell all at home and look little higher; I was still poring either on my sins or wants, or examining my sincerity; but now, though I am greatly convinced of the need of heart-acquaintance and imployment, yet I see more need of a higher work, and that I should look oftener upon Christ and God and heaven, than upon my own heart.'[39]

INTERCESSION

'Intercession' was not used by the Puritans with as wide a meaning as is familiar to us. William Ames, for instance, defines it 'as a peculiar manner of deprecation, namely when that evill which we desire to be removed is placed in some injury done by men'.[40]

Prayer for others, however, was an important part of the Puritan's task. 'Those who only pray for themselves', says William Gouge, 'are most reprehensible.'[41] The more rigid Calvinists found that their doctrine of election created difficulties here. Lewis Bayly could only pray: 'Give thy Gospel a free and joyful passage through the world, for the conversion of those who belong to thine election and kingdom.'[42] William Perkins raises the question 'whether we may pray for al men or no', and decides 'wee may if al men or al mankinde be taken distributively or severally. For there is no particular country, kingdome, towne, person, but we may make prayers for it . . . and though men bee devils incarnate, yet for anything we know they may belong to the election of God: except they sin against the Holy Ghost, which sin is very seldom and very hardly discerned of men. . . . We

---

[38] *Practice of Piety*, p. 130.
[39] Baxter, *Autobiography* (Everyman edn), p. 113, quoted W. O. Chadwick, *John Cassin*, p. 97.
[40] *Marrow of Divinity*, p. 252.
[41] *Workes*, I.182.
[42] *Practice of Piety*, p. 121.

G

may not pray for all men if all men or all mankinde be taken collectively, that is if al men be considered wholly together as they make one body or company and be taken as we say in grosse. For in this body or masse of mankinde there be some whom God in his last judgement hath refused, whose salvation, by prayer shall never be obtained.'[43] So William Ames, while he insists that we neither pray for the dead nor for the salvation of all the living ('because we know the contrary is determined by God'), is sure that no particular living person should be rejected from 'the communion of our prayers neither for any enmity nor for conjectures or probable signs of reprobation'.[44] William Gouge agrees 'that the ground of prayer is the judgement of charity, not of certainty'. Even the Pope, as a man, may be prayed for! Gouge quotes with approval the petition of the Litany: 'That it may please thee to have mercy upon all men.'[45]

The order of praying for others, says Gouge, should be the order of love. The saints come first, for they are the nearest to God who is love, and we are united with them in the Spirit and Body of Christ. Ministers and magistrates come second. Like the prayer for the Church militant in the Prayer Book Communion Service, all the Puritan models are full of petitions for those in authority. In accordance with New Testament teaching, it is believed that by their office in God's stead, and as guardians of public welfare, they are in the position to do most good. Only then do we remember our personal friends, and above all our families, especially husbands and wives; after that 'strangers', which for Gouge means 'all sorts and conditions of men'. Finally, at Christ's express command, we are to pray for our enemies.[46]

We are to ask for others what we desire for ourselves—the conversion of those not yet called, the establishment of those who are called, the forgiveness of their sins, the healing of the sick, and the deliverance of the oppressed.

Thomas Goodwin is a little more cautious in his attitude to prayer for those who may be blotted out of God's book. He concludes that though our prayers cannot avail for the rejected, the act of praying may be good for us. 'If we have prayed long for those whom God intendeth not mercy unto, he will in the end

[43] *Workes*, I.347-8.
[44] *Marrow of Divinity*, p. 252.
[45] *Workes*, I.182-91, from which all quotations are taken.
[46] 'A noble singularity of our religion' (Isaac Watts, *Guide to Prayer*).

cast them out of our prayers and hearts, and take our hearts off praying for them. . . .'[47] He may also answer our prayers and compensate by giving us new friends to pray for, a David for a Saul, or an Isaac for an Ishmael. We cannot pray too much for the Church. God 'never revealed his love to Moses more than when he prayed most for God's people'.

We may be thankful that Gouge at any rate is less inclined to limit the scope of prayer than many of his contemporaries. But it may be some extenuation of these Puritans that the prayer of the Church has not traditionally been as universalist as that of the Lord who sought the forgiveness of His torturers. Neither the canon of the Mass, nor the Anglican rite of Holy Communion normally makes mention of reprobates or intercedes for all men. The Good Friday Collects are something of an exception, though one of them seems to lack the spirit of self-identification with sinners which would seem to be most Christian; for they stand over against 'Jews, Turks, infidels and hereticks' and invoke a divine mercy, which according to the Roman Liturgy does not exclude 'even perfidious Jews'.[48] The intercessions of Lancelot Andrewes's *Preces Privatae* are generally more comprehensive, omitting none. A touch of Arminianism breaks the bonds of a logic which otherwise restricts men by nature compassionate. Yet if sheer fidelity to premises narrowed the intercessions of some Puritans, they had a tremendous faith in the all-prevailing prayer of Christ for those who are His. Thomas Goodwin can say: 'Men have been cast out of good and holy men's prayers as Saul out of Samuel's, and the people of Israel out of Jeremiah's but never out of Christ's; the smoke of his incense ascends for ever, and he will intercede to the utmost till he hath saved to the utmost. He will never give over, but will lie in the dust for thee, or he will perfect and procure thy salvation.'[49] The real work of intercession is Christ's and only in Him can any prayer of ours win acceptance.

THE INTERCESSOR

The inevitable and supreme condition of Christian prayer is

[47] *Works*, III.368. Other quotations ibid., pp. 366-70.
[48] A. R. George, *Communion with God in the New Testament*, pp. 48-9; cf. also the *Geneva Prayer Book* of Calvin for a similar self-consciousness.
[49] *Works*, IV.91.

that it must be offered in the name of Jesus. He is the one
Mediator whose Intercession presents our prayers at the Throne
of Grace. We must approach God through Jesus, because the
Tremendous Majesty is too awful for our contemplation. 'Thou
canst not see my face: for man shall not see me and live.'[50]
Divine Justice can but destroy the ungodly, but 'while we were yet
sinners Christ died for us'. Thus, says Richard Sibbes, like Jacob's
sons going to Joseph, we must in going to God 'take Benjamin
with us', that is our Christ. 'Be sure not to go to a naked God:
for so he is a consuming fire, but go to him in the mediation of
him whom he loves. . . .'[51] Our daily devotion, our frequent
confession of 'slips and errors' must be to offer Christ to God.
No other mediator, whether he be priest or saint, is possible.
Sibbes suggests words in the spirit of which we can thus offer
Christ. 'Behold, Lord, thy chosen servant that thou hast chosen
to be my mediator my saviour, my all in all to me, he is a mediator
and saviour of thine own choosing, thou canst not refuse thine
own choice; if thou look upon me, there is nothing but matter of
unworthiness, but look upon him whom thou hast chosen my
head, and my saviour.'[52]

This reminds us of the words which Martin Luther records as
the advice given him by his confessor Staupitz, which find frequent
echo in his writings. He was distressed at the thought of predestination, and Staupitz said to him: 'In the wounds of Christ
is predestination understood and found and nowhere else. . . . The
Father is too high, therefore He says: I will give a way by which

[50] Exodus 33²⁰.

[51] *Works*, I.13.

[52] ibid., p. 10. More than a century later, P. Doddridge echoes Sibbes's words: 'Be
assured you must not apply yourselves immediately to God as absolutely, or in himself
considered, in the Neglect of a Mediator. It will neither be acceptable to him, nor
safe for you to rush into his presence, without any regard for his own Son whom he has
appointed to introduce sinners to him' (*Rise and Progress of Religion* (1798 edn), p. 81).
Watts has prayers of his own in similar strain. 'Lord let my sins be forgiven for the
sake of the love which thy Son beareth to thee; for the sake of his humble state, when
he took flesh upon him that he might look like a sinner and be made a sacrifice,
though himself free from sin; for the sake of his perfect and painful obedience, which
has given compleat Honour to the Law; for the sake of the Curse which he bore, and
the Death which he suffered, which hath glorified thine Authority, and honoured thy
justice more than was possible for my sins to have affronted it; remember his dying
groans; remember his agonies when the hour of darkness was upon him, and let not
the powers of darkness prevail over me; remember the day when thou stoodest afar
from thine own Son, he cried out as one forsaken of God, let me have thine everlasting
presence with me, and, let me never be forsaken, since thy Son hath born that punishment' (*Guide to Prayer* (1722 edn), p. 17).

man may come to Me; ... in Christ you shall find what and who I am, and what I will; otherwise you will not find it either in heaven or on earth.'[53] Could it be that, like Luther, a Puritan would find in the mediation of Christ release from the self-tortures of double predestination? The experience of a Bunyan, to whom Luther's *Galatians* meant so much, suggests that it could.

Luther does not, however, in his own theological formulations, which leave beyond doubt his insistence on the perfect unity of the Father and the Son in the work of redemption, allow himself such dangerous statements as that of the eighteenth-century Zinzendorf: 'God, the Father of our Lord Jesus Christ, is not our immediate Father ... he becoming our Father only by the reconciliation, and faith in the mediation of his Son. . . . Therefore we have properly to do with no one else than with the Son, our Mediator.'[54]

There was no conflict in Puritan thought between the intercession of Christ and the purpose of the Father. Thomas Goodwin, in *Christ Set Forth*, expounds with tremendous conviction the unity of the Father and the Son. It is because Christ's heart is one with the Father in all things that He is our Mediator. Goodwin's view of the Passion and Work of Christ is that found in St John's Gospel and the Epistle to the Hebrews. Christ's intercession makes our justification actual: 'He shed his blood on the Cross on earth, but he sprinkleth it as a priest from heaven.'[55] Moreover, it makes our justification continual: 'We owe our standing in grace every moment to his sitting in heaven and interceding every moment.'[56] Like creation, the work was finished once for all, yet still goes on. And Christ's intercession makes our justification secure. It is not as though God needed Christ as a sign to remind Him of His mercy. Rather is Christ given to us as a surety, like the rainbow of old, the eternal remembrance of God's love and pardon.[57]

Thus we need no other Mediator. 'Shall we run to saints

---

[53] *Tischreden* 12 nr. 19, quoted Philip S. Watson, *Let God be God*, pp. 19-20. This teaching is found in the medieval *Stimulus Amoris* in which the soul considers what to do 'if I be ordained to reprobation', and finally declares: 'I know what I will doe, I will go and hide myself in the cavernes of his wounds, and there remain quietly' (quoted L. L. Martz, *The Poetry of Mediation*, p. 159).

[54] Quoted R. A. Knox, *Enthusiasm*, p. 408, from Stinstra, *Essay in Fanaticism*, App., pp. 53-4. For Luther, see Watson, op. cit., pp. 116 ff.

[55] *Works*, IV.64.

[56] ibid., pp. 64-5.

[57] ibid.

for mediation; to the virgin Mary and others for intercession which is part of Christ's office? There is no mention in Scripture of them for this purpose, but behold my servant whom I have chosen.'[58]

In Christ alone can we truly pray, because in Him alone are we declared and made righteous. 'An unregenerate man', says Preston, 'may frame a prayer as well as a holy man', but, 'our sinnes outcry our prayers till our persons be right.'[59] Prayer in the Name of Jesus is ethical prayer as distinct from demented incantation, that is, it is prayer made ethical by union with His perfect righteousness.

THE HOLY SPIRIT IN PRAYER

The Puritans found themselves confronted by two verses from the eighth chapter of Romans to which they gave full weight. The one declares that Christ ever lives to make intercession for us, the other that we have also an Intercessor within—'The Spirit itself maketh intercession for us'.

John Owen deals with the problem of this dual intercession in expounding Zechariah 12[10]: 'I will pour upon the House of David and upon the inhabitants of Jerusalem the Spirit of grace and of supplications.'[60] The Holy Spirit cannot make intercession for Himself, else would He be less than God; nor can He interpose in heaven on our behalf, for that is the priestly office of Christ. His intercession is—using the scholastic term of Owen—'efficient'; that is, He works in us, stirring us up to pray, and He makes us able to pray. Richard Sibbes teaches similarly: 'The Gospel breeds love in us to God, and hath the Spirit together with it working a blessed frame of sanctification, whereby we are disposed to do every good duty.'[61] Thus it is by the strength and assistance of the Holy Spirit that we are enabled, albeit groaningly, to approach God through Christ. The Spirit brings us to Christ, and Christ to God. He is the Spirit of Christ, the legacy of the Lord now in Glory, Christ's 'shaliach' in the earth, to dispose us to all virtue and turn our hearts to Him who pleads before the throne. John Preston defines prayer as 'an expression or offering of those

---

[58] R. Sibbes, *Works*, I.10.   [59] *Saint's Daily Exercise*, p. 103 margin.
[60] *Works*, IV.254 ff. Gouge also treats of the same text, *Workes*, I.229 ff.
[61] *Works*, I.24.

holy and good dispositions to God, that arise from the spirit or the regenerate part, in the name of Jesus Christ'.[62] The Spirit alone makes possible those good and concentrated dispositions which are as a burning-glass held up to the sun, and bring light and heat to the soul from God.

The Spirit who thus inspires our prayer is also the Spirit of adoption whereby we cry 'Abba Father'. That simple cry of the child is true prayer. As John Owen declares: 'There is no more required unto prayer either way but our crying, "Abba Father"— that is, the making our requests known unto him as our father in Christ—with supplications and thanksgivings, according as our state and occasions do require.'[63] Dr Nuttall shows that for Puritans of all parties the basis of prayer in the Spirit is the conviction of the Fatherhood of God. We may borrow his quotation from the Congregationalist Walter Cradock:

'It is ordinary with the Saints, that they have a little adoption, they can cry Abba Father a little, and low and at sometimes: but there is a great deale of the spirit of bondage mingled with it, there are sometimes feares, secret whisperings in the heart. . . . Now in the New Testament, we should labour for a full spirit of adoption. . . . If thou come below this, if thou call on God with feare, & canst not cry abba, abba, that is as much as daddie, daddie, as our babes used to say, if thou doe not come so high, thou art spoiled, and undone, desire God to teach thee this lesson also.'[64]

The same Cradock also singles out four functions of the 'power of the Spirit': (1) In dictating a world of prayer to us. We may make forms of prayer; only the Spirit can make spiritual petitions. (2) In supplying us when we pray not. (3) In teaching us inwardly. (4) In working our works in and for us.[65]

The Puritans do not despise the human understanding. The Spirit helps us to pray by crowning our natural aspirations. John Owen does not think the Spirit inspires our supplications by an immediate Divine revelation as he inspired the Prophets of old, who did not fully comprehend His meaning, but rather by giving voice and action to—indeed making actual—our desires and

[62] *Saint's Daily Exercise*, pp. 2, 3.
[63] *Works*, IV.269.
[64] *Glad Tydings from Heaven*, pp. 40-3, quoted Nuttall, pp. 63-4.
[65] *Sermon on Ephesians* 2²⁰.

requests.[66] Thus Owen denies 'Enthusiasm'. Bunyan asserts that the understanding must be occupied in prayer as well as the Spirit. We must grasp with our minds, our needs, God's willingness to save us, the way to Him, the largeness of the promises. We must also learn to wrestle with God, and to know what to pray for, and how to pray on each occasion. But this for Bunyan, as for St Paul, is to be distinguished from the work of the Spirit in prayer. 'I will pray with the Spirit and I will pray with the understanding also.'[67]

[66] *Works*, IV.263. Cf. H. Watkin-Jones, *The Holy Spirit from Arminius to Wesley* (London 1929), pp. 175-6.
[67] *A Discourse Touching Prayer*, *Works* I.632-4.

The Love of Jesus, like the power of light, may be wrongly analysed, but its width and potency are none the less for our failure to explain them. It is one of the powers of Nature; it is enough that it is there.

CHARLES BIGG

Of all tears, they are the best that are made by the Blood of Christ; and of all joy, that is the sweetest that is mixed with mourning over Christ. Oh! 'tis a goodly thing to be on our knees, with Christ in our arms before God.

JOHN BUNYAN

His dying crimson, like a robe
Spreads o'er his body on the tree,
Then am I dead to all the globe,
And all the globe is dead to me.

ISAAC WATTS

CHAPTER SIX

THE PRAYER OF LOVE

MEDITATION AND MENTAL PRAYER

THE Puritans laid great store by meditation, but it is important to notice differences of usage of the term in their writings, and to try to trace the influence of ideas from the Counter-Reformation and indeed medieval spirituality. Thomas Hooker defines meditation as 'a serious intention of the mind, whereby we come to search out the truth and settle it effectually upon the heart'.[1] He uses St Bernard's word 'consideration', and like Paul Baynes employs the Salesian metaphor of mastication. But he chiefly applies it to self-examination.

A familiar feature of the guides to godliness is the suggestion of serious and profitable thought to accompany the simple tasks of daily life. The bed is always to remind the sleeper of his grave, his rising of the resurrection from the dead. Should he hear the cock crow, he must remember Peter's denial and penitence with many tears. The putting on of clothes is to carry the mind back to man's primeval innocence and fallen shame. The sun streaming through the windows is to be a sign of the Sun of Righteousness, risen with healing in His wings.[2]

It is easy to see the weaknesses and exaggerations of all this. Earthly and natural things become almost utilitarian—their pre-eminent virtues being in the lessons they teach—and we are in danger of finding a sermon for ourselves, and still more for others, in every stone. In his introduction to the 1948 Yale University Press edition of Jonathan Edwards's *Images or Shadows of Divine Things*, Perry Miller contrasts the Puritan and Anglican traditions in their mental attitude to the natural world. The Puritan is less of an 'imagist' and more of an 'allegorist' than the Anglican, less content to admire nature for its own sake; he is for ever seeking

---

[1] *Application of Redemption*, II.210.
[2] Based on passages from Bayly and Downame. In the *Evangelische Theologie* (September 1951), Erich Beyreuther has an article on the Origins of Pietism, in which he notes the influence of Bayly and Southam on Francke, and quotes from Francke's *Sermons* (1713) a passage similar to the above.

the Divine Purpose of the blasted oak, the moral lesson of the withered rose, even seriously trying, as did the American, Cotton Mather, to 'make the objects of the summer subservient to the interests of Piety'.[3] John Dod, for instance, says that God created heaven and earth in six days and not in less, 'Because we might have a fitter occasion and be better moved to consider of the severall creatures. For if he had folded all up in an houre then it had not been so easie and plaine for our meditation.'[4] We have only to contrast what cock-crow signified to Bayly and Downame with Henry Vaughan's poem on the same subject, to understand that the Puritans might so meditate on nature as to see nothing but the parable of man's redemption, and be guilty of that anthropocentricity with which Pourrat charges Protestantism.[5] But Dod's words are susceptible of another interpretation, for they were written in the age which was the nursing mother of modern science. May they not betoken an interest in nature which could inspire a scientist to search out her secrets with reverence? Richard Baxter teaches a meditation upon nature which is much more sacramental:

'You can open your Bible, and read there of God and of glory, oh learn to open the creatures and to open the several passages of providence and to read of God and glory there. Certainly by such a skilful industrious improvement, we might have a fuller taste of Christ and heaven in every bit of bread that we eat and in every draught of beer we drink, than most men have in the use of the Sacrament. . . . Thus you may see, what advantage to a heavenly life every condition and

---

[3] Cited Perry Miller, op. cit., p. 14.
[4] *Ten Commandments*, p. 157.
[5]   *Father of Lights! what Sunnie seed,*
              What glance of day hast thou confined
            Into this bird? To all the breed
              This busy ray thou has assign'd.
            Their magnetisme works all night,
            And dreams of Paradise and light.

                    .   .

            If joyes, and hopes, and earnest throws,
              And hearts whose Pulse beats still for light,
            Are given to birds; who, but thee knows
              A love sick soul's exalted flight?
            Can souls be track'd by any eye
            But his, who gave them wings to fly?

H. Vaughan, 'Cock-Crowing', *Works* (Oxford 1914), II.488. See Pourrat, *Christian Spirituality*, III.70.

creature doth afford us, if we had but hearts to apprehend them.'[6]

The quotation is from Baxter's *The Saint's Everlasting Rest*. Professor Louis L. Martz claims that this work marks a new stage of English Puritanism in which meditation shows signs of the influence of Catholic models. But it is possible that Martz is ignoring Baxter's predecessors.[7] Baxter uses Jean Gerson (1363-1429), but if we would go to the sources of Lewis Bayly's *Practice of Piety*, we must not ignore the *Spiritual Exercises* of Ignatius Loyola. Some of Bayly's extended meditations might well follow the Ignatian advice to see, hear, and smell the horror of the damned, for example. Bayly opens hell's mouth for us as though he were making aloud, and for our sakes, a Jesuit meditation.[8]

There is also frequent use by the Puritans before Baxter of colloquy and soliloquy. Paul Baynes in his letters counsels these, and reviews the descent of the method from David through Augustine, Anselm, and Bernard. Baxter, of course, says very much the same—forty years later! 'How oft doth David intermix these in his Psalms, sometimes pleading with his soul and sometimes with God.'[9] But earlier still, Henry Smith, in the midst of confession, and in adoration of the Divine and Compassionate Majesty, slips into a remonstrance with his soul, reminding her of her privileges, costly redemption and many foes, reproaching her at great length with her lifeless ingratitude, and then crying 'But why do I utter my voice, or strive to make a dead carcase move? Oh! quicken thou me, that art the fountain of life, and call out of heaven, thy dwelling place, that my wandering soul may hear the voice of her shepherd, and follow thee whithersoever thou leadest, nay, of thy tender compassion take me upon thy shoulders and carry me gently into thy fold again.'[10] It is in this idiom of soliloquy that, as we shall see, the Puritans yearn after the Divine Love.

---

[6] *Works*, XXIII.300-1. (It is interesting to find this kind of Sacramentalism not related to specific Communion meditations, where the emphasis, as we have seen, was mostly soteriological.)

[7] *The Poetry of Meditation*, p. 174. For an account of Gerson, see Pourrat *Christian Spirituality*, II.268 ff.

[8] *The Practice of Piety*, pp. 48-9; cf. Ignatius Loyola, op. cit., p. 67.

[9] *Works*, XXIII.372; cf. R. Sibbes, *Works*, I.197-9.

[10] *Works*, II.458.

Isaac Ambrose, as well as Richard Baxter, distinguishes the types of meditation. He classifies them as Sudden or Set, Occasional or Solemn, Extemporal or Deliberate.[11] Ambrose has three definitions of the more intensive kind of meditation. It is 'a deep and earnest musing upon some point of Christian instruction to the strengthening of us against the flesh, world and devil; and to the leading us forward to the Kingdom of Heaven'; or 'a steadfast bending of the mind to some spiritual matter, discoursing of it with ourselves till we bring it to some profitable issue'; or 'A separating of our thoughts and affections from the world; a drawing forth of all our graces in order, and exercising of each of them on its proper object, and holding them to this, till we perceive success, and till the world doth thrive and prosper in our hand'. This meditation must be at a stated time and frequent, to prevent shyness in the presence of God and failure to advance in His knowledge.

William Gouge approves of mental prayer, a seventeenth-century term according to Professor Martz, and finds scriptural precedent in the stories of Nehemiah, Moses, and Hannah.[12] John Owen attacks mental prayer 'as pretended unto by some in the Church of Rome'.[13] He is afraid that it may result in the abandonment of reason, and the release of unrestrained fancy. He calls it 'a kind of Purgatory in devotion'.[14] He anticipates our modern dialectical theologians by attributing its vogue to the unfortunate synthesis of neo-Platonism and Christianity, and he regards it as unscriptural, since our Lord himself not only taught a form of words, but prayed, 'with strong crying and tears'. The mind and words so act and react upon each other, that while words are the children of thoughts, they also inspire thoughts and strengthen good dispositions. 'There is a recoiling of efficacy, if I may so speak, in deep impressions on the affections, from the words that are made use of to express those affections by.'[15] Mental prayer may easily lead to blasphemous individual claims and to unholy babblings; it does not edify the Church and leads to disputes as to the validity of the mystical experience. It is not prayer in the scriptural sense, and it may disregard the mediation of Christ, seeking to make God all in all to the Church before Christ has delivered up to Him the mediatorial kingdom. In

[11] *Works*, p. 117.   [12] *Workes*, I.208.   [13] *Works*, IV.328 ff.
[14] ibid., p. 338.   [15] ibid., p. 331.

other words, like the doctrine of Transubstantiation, it may attempt to bypass the Parousia.

Owen, however, does not condemn 'Holy meditations', and he describes spiritual acts of communion which, although as Bernard of Clairvaux says, '*Rara hora, brevis mora*', 'may be enjoyed in mental or vocal prayer indifferently'. 'The *spiritual intense fixation of the mind,* by contemplation on God in Christ, until the soul be as it were swallowed up in admiration and delight, and being brought unto an utter loss, through the infiniteness of those excellencies which it doth admire and adore, it returns again into its own abasements, out of a sense of its infinite distance from what it would absolutely and eternally embrace, and, withal, the inexpressible rest and satisfaction which the will and affection receive in their approaches unto the eternal Fountain of goodness, are things to be aimed at in prayer, and which, through the riches of divine condescension are frequently enjoyed.' But these are gifts of God, not the achievements of devotional technique. They do not ravish the soul into irrational ecstasy. Rather they fill it in all its faculties with overwhelming joy in the Divine Grace revealed in Christ.

THE DIVINE LOVE

The various kinds of prayer have been analysed with great thoroughness by modern theologians. One of the most famous is Friedrich Heiler, who distinguishes between 'mystical' and 'prophetic' prayer, though in the Preface to the fifth German edition of his book *Das Gebet* he prefers the term 'faith piety' to 'prophetic prayer'. He defines the ambiguous word mysticism as 'that form of intercourse with God in which the world and self are absolutely denied, in which human personality is dissolved, disappears, and is absorbed in the infinite unity of the Godhead'.[16] On the other hand: 'The prophet is a fighter who ever struggles upwards from doubt to assurance, from tormenting uncertainty to absolute security of life, from despondency to fresh courage of the soul, from fear to hope, from a depressing consciousness of guilt to the blessed experience of grace and salvation.' 'If "love" and "union" are the central conceptions of mysticism, "faith" is the watchword of prophetic religion.'

Dr Kenneth Kirk subscribes to Heiler's distinction, though he

[16] *Prayer*, p. 136.

misunderstands its author's position.[17] He is anxious to give what
he calls contemplative prayer (which is perhaps a more satis-
factory term to apply to Christian piety than mystical) pride of
place over prophetic, and also to liberate Christians from the
tyrannies of the idea of prayer as 'request and response'.[18]

But we must not let these analyses blind us to the fact, which
both Heiler and Kirk recognize, that in true Christian prayer faith
and love will both be apparent. We have earlier quoted Gouge's
definition that prayer is 'a right opening of the desire of the heart
to God'.[19] The utterance of this desire may well be the petition
of child-like trust, or the agonized asking for the recovery of a
loved one from sickness, or for courage to face death. But by its
very ardour and passion it will resemble that desire of which the
Psalmist speaks when he says: 'My soul thirsteth for God, for the
living God; When shall I come and appear before God?' The
prayer of faith, of that trust in the Father which batters heaven's
door, leads on to the prayer of love which seeks not only God's
gifts but himself, and cries amid the request for daily bread: 'Thy
will be done.'

The Christian idea of love also has had its analysts, notably
the Swedish theologian, Anders Nygren. He distinguishes between
agape—the spontaneous, uncaused love of God Himself—and
eros—the highest human love, the sublimation of all earthly desires
in the quest for Heaven. The one is love in the biblical sense; the
other derives from Plato, and is united with *agape* by Augustine.
'The result is the emergence of a new concept of love, summed up
in the word *caritas*. Between two things so different as *agape* and
eros no real synthesis was possible, but only a relative synthesis;
and such is *caritas*. On this synthesis the Middle Ages lived;
Medieval Christianity is throughout *caritas* religion.'[20] The
Renaissance and Reformation separate *eros* and *agape* again, and
Luther is as remarkable for his rediscovery of the Christian idea
of love, as for his great battle for justification *sola fide*.

The weakness of Nygren's thesis is clear. Not only does he
fail to explain at all convincingly our Lord's great commandment that we should love God with our whole being, but he

[17] *The Vision of God*, pp. 414 ff. See A. R. George, *Communion with God in the New Testament*, p. 10.
[18] *Beauty and Bands*, p. 31.
[19] See p. 70, *supra*.
[20] A. Nygren, *Agape and Eros* (1932 edn), Part I, p. 39.

neglects the Johannine idea of love as *philia* and is compelled to recognize that the *eros* idea is found in the very Johannine writings which, together with Paul's hymn to love, 'have stamped the idea of *agape* on the mind of Christendom'.[21] All Nygren writes about the divine *agape* passes without question—here he unfolds the very heart of the Gospel—but can we rightly regard as extraneous all language of human desire and longing? Does not Nygren deal too much in abstract ideas whether Pauline or Platonist, and pay insufficient regard to the human personality whether as lover or beloved?[22] In any Christian life there will be the divine *agape* completely undeserved, the free grace of God; but there will be the ordinary human desires too, capable of serving selfish ends or of being transformed by God's love. It is surely *eros* of which *agape* takes hold, and God himself is the true satisfaction of our desires as well as our Saviour from sin, though we must not exploit Him either way. Luther's language about the 'ladder' is a problem for Nygren.[23] How right Luther is in insisting that we cannot 'climb up into the majesty of God' by our own schemes or efforts, that Christ is indeed the only ladder! How much more evangelical is this explanation of Jacob's dream, which we have already noted in the margin of the Geneva Bible, than that of St Francis of Sales.[24] But while it is true that there are those who have made the Cross itself a scheme of salvation, the centre of an anthropocentric system, Luther's plain words seem to mean (*pace* Nygren) that while all human ways of ascent are false, by this way, Christ, we can rise to heaven.

Quite simply, the Puritans held that as grace elevates reason, so it transforms human love; our ardour and passion may be directed to worldly and sensual objects or to God who first loved

---

[21] Nygren, ibid., p. 117. For criticisms of Nygren see J. Burnaby, *Amor Dei*, e.g. pp. 15 ff, 92 ff, 121 f, 275 f, though note Philip S. Watson's answer to them, as they relate to Nygren's treatment of Luther in *Let God be God*, Chap. 2; cf. M. C. D'Arcy, *The Mind and Heart of Love*, esp. Chap. 2.

[22] Contrast Burnaby's fine analysis of human love, *Amor Dei*, pp. 301 ff.

[23] *Agape and Eros*, Part 2, II.489 ff and notes.

[24] *Jacob's Ladder in Protestant and Catholic Typology*. Luther: 'Every ascent to the knowledge of God is perilous except that which is made through the humility of Christ; for this is Jacob's ladder on which the ascent must be made' (quoted Nygren, ibid.); cf. Margin of the Geneva Bible: 'Christ is the ladder whereby God and man are joined together, by whom the angels minister unto us; all graces by him are joined to us, and we by him ascend into heaven'; cf. also Bunyan: ' . . . Christ is Jacob's ladder that reacheth up to heaven and he that refuseth to go up by this ladder thither will scarce get up so high' (*The Jerusalem Sinner Saved, Works*, I.103); John 1⁵¹. Contrast Francis of Sales, for whom the two sides of the ladder are prayer and the sacraments, and the rungs the progressive degrees of charity (*Introduction*).

us. In his short essay, *Mount Ebal: a Heavenly Treatise of Divine Love*, John Preston distinguishes natural, sinful, and spiritual love. The first is instanced by the love of parent and child; the second is a worse-than-animal passion, since it breeds evil habits in the soul; the third is given only by the Holy Spirit and leads us to desire holy things for themselves. It is the same motive power of the soul throughout.

Preston uses two figures to describe the operation of love. He compares love to the rudder of a ship; it is a steadying, guiding power. But love is also a fire: 'As fire begets fire, so doth love beget love.'[25] As he writes elsewhere: 'If thou be in Christ, there goes out a virtue from him that stamps upon thy heart this holy affection that breedes in thee this holy fire of love, so that thy heart cleaves to him, thou lovest him with as true, with as genuine, as naturall and as sensible love as thou lovest any friend; as thou lovest any creature in the world.'[26]

We may compare with this what Henry Scougal, the Scottish Episcopalian, was later to write in his *Life of God in the Soul of Man*: 'Love is that powerful and prevalent passion, by which all the faculties and inclinations of the soul are determined, and on which both its perfection and its happiness depend.'[27] Therefore, says Scougal, in words which would horrify Nygren, our love is the 'worthiest present' we can offer God. 'Those unlimited submissions, which would debase the soul if directed to any other will exalt and ennoble it when placed here: those claims and words of love are infinitely more glorious than liberty itself; this slavery is more noble than all the empires in the world.'[28] Love here is the *philia* 'in which Aristotle discovered the richest endowment of human personality—a mutual relation, a bond which links two centres of consciousness in one'.[29] This is the love of the last discourses of the Fourth Gospel. It is this which St Francis of Sales glorifies in his *Traité de L'Amour de Dieu*.[30]

And Preston knows something of the rapture of divine love.[31] He is not content merely to analyse; he yearns—'pants' is his word as it is the Psalmist's—after the love of Jesus, that it may

[25] *Mount Ebal*, pp. 10, 24.
[26] *A Preparation to the Lord's Supper*, p. 94.
[27] op. cit., p. 31.
[28] ibid., p. 34.
[29] J. Burnaby, *Amor Dei*, p. 18.
[30] See Burnaby, ibid., pp. 277-86; M. C. D'Arcy, *Mind and Heart of Love*, p. 112.
[31] *Mount Ebal*, p. 23.

be no mere historical fact but a living reality in his soul. To the 1640 edition of his *Five Sermons on the Divine Love* he appends, *The Soliloquy of a Devout Soul to Christ, Panting after the Love of the Lord Jesus:*

I have hid myselfe from thee as Adam, yet thou hast pierced through the darke cloud and loved me. . . . Thou hast often showed me thy riches, and I have loved them; but Oh shew me thyselfe that I may love thee. . . .

. . . If I looke to Mount Tabor, I see thee in glory, and I cannot but love thee for that. If I looke to the garden, I see thee lying on the cold ground sweating drops of bloud for me, and I cannot but love thee for that. If I looke to Golgotha, I see thee nailed to the Cross, and thy heart broached that I may drinke thy bloud and live, and I cannot but love thee for that. If I looke to Mount Olivet I see thee ascending farre above all heavens, and I cannot but love thee for that also. Indeed in Tabor thou hadst visible glory but it soon vanished; in the garden and Golgotha thou hadst little visible beauty why I should desire thee; and in Olivet thou wast quite carried out of my sight. If then thou liest for me nowhere else what hope have I to love thee, Oh thou to be beloved of all. Art thou not in the tents of the shepherds? Dost thou not walke in the midst of the golden candlesticks? Dost thou not dwell in the hearts of men by faith? Oh let me see thee here below in the Church and in myselfe.

Sin is the one obstacle, Preston continues, as he clamours to be made perfect in love. 'I finde the filth of domineering sinne in some measure washed from the windows of my soul that the beams of thy glory may pierce it and draw my love after thee.'[32]

In *Mount Ebal*, Preston continues by asking three questions. The first is 'Do we love Christ?' and we are told to test our love by examining the motives of our good deeds. Do they spring from love or custom? Do we love Christ's company in Word and Sacrament, do we long for His appearing, do we feed His flock? Love will be content with nothing but love again. The vision of Christ's beauty will be its supreme desire. But we love Him if we love our brethren, if we speak well of Him whenever we are able, if we 'linger and hang after him', and renew in the Sacrament the Covenant of Love.

The next question is 'Why love Jesus?' And the answer is

[32] Printed at the conclusion (pp. 89 ff) of J. Preston, *A Heavenly Treatise of the Divine Love of Christ*, in *Five Sermons* (London 1640).

simply an elaboration of the Johannine 'Because he first loved us'.
But thirdly 'How can we get love?' There are two chief ways—
prayer and desire. Prayer prevails with God to cast out sin, and
like the Magdalen, 'forgiven greatly, we greatly love'. Prayer
also makes us familiar with God, and familiarity does not breed
contempt among friends. (We notice here how the prayer of
faith and the prayer of love are one.) Desire for the love of Christ
means that we shall give ear to preaching, and seek to know God's
truth. We shall be humbled to repentance for our sins. We cannot
love Christ if we do not know Him, nor if we love the world.
There is a sense in which we must love only Christ. Our love for
others will be in a sense a different love, because we love them in
Him.[33]

THE SACRED HUMANITY AND THE PASSION

Preston bids us love Jesus as Lord, Saviour, and Messiah, but
he does not direct us to the events of Christ's saving work quite as
do some of his contemporaries. As his soliloquy reveals, he desires
an immediacy of communion more close than credal and
historical knowledge sometimes gives.

It is a remarkable fact, that before St Bernard of Clairvaux,
devotion to the Sacred Humanity had not been conspicuous. At
least it was not expressed in writing with the tenderness and
rapture that henceforth became the vogue. The great Fathers
had a firm sense of history, but we can apply to them, and not
least to Augustine, what Dr Prestige says of Ignatius of Antioch:
'He never sought to traverse in the opposite direction the road by
which Christ ascended into heaven, to return to Golgotha and
watch the sacred blood drip to the ground.'[34] True as that may
be, there are differences of opinion as to what Ignatius meant when
he said in his letter to the Romans: 'My Love (*Eros*) is crucified.'
Dr Prestige, like Bishop Lightfoot, regards *Eros* here as meaning
'lower nature', or as Wesley says, 'creature-love'. Dr Bigg
believes that Origen was right when he translated the Greek
Eros by the Latin '*Amor*', and obviously referred it to Christ.
William Perkins follows Origen's interpretation of Ignatius and

---

[33] The above is an exposition of J. Preston, *Mount Ebal*, pp. 23-8; cf. Burnaby on
love of neighbour in Augustine, *Amor Dei*, pp. 127-37.

[34] *Fathers and Heretics*, p. 377. Popular devotion however may have been more
interested in historical details, e.g. Helena, Mother of Constantine (died *c.* 330),
and Venantius Fortunatus (*c.* 530-609).

says: 'We must therefore labour above all, following the Martyr Ignatius, who said that Christ, his love, was crucified.'[35]

From the twelfth century the road back to Calvary was often traversed, and although Bernard himself intended it to be but the way to the heights of mystical experience, he inaugurated for ordinary Christians a new piety of the Crucified. And (*pace* Dr Prestige) the English Reformation by no means dethroned St Bernard. Calvin, it is true, and his professed followers give the impression of a colder piety, but the Bernardine tradition is often mingled with it. We have noted above the similarity between Ignatius Loyola and the Puritan guides to godliness, and the Jesuit is in some ways a revival of Bernard. The seventeenth century saw English editions of several works attributed to Bernard,[36] some obviously Puritan, and with sundry amendments and prunings.

A Roman Catholic treatise of the same tradition, which circulated in English, and which seems to have influenced the Metaphysical Poets[37] among others, was Bishop Guevara's *Mount Calvary*. The Bishop is described on the title page as 'Preacher, Chronicler, Councellor to Charles V'. His book is in two parts: first, a lengthy series of meditations on the details of the Passion; and second, an equally long commentary on the Seven Words from the Cross. Typology and patristic references abound, indeed run riot. Here is one chapter heading: 'How they did naile Christ his right hand, and how in Solomon's house there was no hammer heard, and that the flesh on the Sonne of God was all knocked with hammers.'[38] There are many soliloquies of the crucified and an emphasis on the physical horrors of the Passion and Death. There is apostrophe of the sacred flesh, holy blood, cruel spear, and wood of the Cross: 'All haile O precious Crosse, I reverence thee O holy wood.'[39]

Professor William Haller, with whom Professor Martz agrees,

---

[35] *Workes*, I.752; cf. C. Bigg, *The Christian Platonists of Alexandria*, pp. viii ff, and W. R. Inge, *Christian Mysticism*, p. 110. It is most interesting (and revealing) to see that Charles Wesley uses *both* interpretations, a point which seems to have escaped Henry Bett, *The Hymns of Methodism in their Literary Relations* (Third edn (1956), p. 98). Contrast *MHB*, No. 229[5] with *MHB* No. 186.

[36] See Helen C. White, *English Devotional Literature*, pp. 69 ff.

[37] Itrat-Husain, *The Mystical Element in the Metaphysical Poets* (Edinburgh, 1948), p. 177.

[38] op. cit., p. 206; cf. medieval devotions as described in P. Pourrat, *Christian Spirituality*, II.319 ff.

[39] op. cit., p. 414; cf. p. 349.

has said that 'the symbolism of the Nativity and Passion came to mean little to the Puritan saints'.[40] This is not true without some qualification. Though Bunyan's Christian does not linger at the Cross, Bunyan himself does.[41] Isaac Ambrose's *Looking unto Jesus* has some similarity to Bishop Guevara's book, though he meditates upon the whole work of Christ from Creation to the last day, and thus sets Calvary in its context of the universal purpose of God in Christ. It is because the Puritans do not separate Christ Crucified from Christ Triumphant that Martz can so misunderstand them as to say that they meditate more on Christ's 'official role' than on His personality.[42] The Puritans did not use the Crucifix, at least not the material image, but in their mind's eye they were very conscious of the redemptive sufferings of Christ. Thomas Adams has a sermon on the Passion entitled 'A Crucifixe', but his theme is 'a faire and lively crucifixe, cut by the hand of a most exquisite carver; not to amaze our corporall lights, with a peece of wood, brasse, or stone curiously engraven to the increase of a carnall devotion. But to present to the eye of the conscience the grievous passion and gracious compassion of our Saviour Jesus Christ'.[43]

Nevertheless, in 'the soul's looking unto Jesus in his death' Ambrose bids us accompany Christ over the brook Kidron (whose waters typify God's wrath, man's rage, and the Lord's own sufferings) to the garden, the judgement hall and the tree. Every detail has eternal significance; it is the fulfilment of prophecy; it is also related to our present sin and need:

O my pride! and O my covetousness! O my malice and revenge! and O my unbelief! O my unthankfulness! O my uncharitableness to the needy members of Christ Jesus! Why these were the rout, these were they that led and dragged and drew Jesus (as it were) by the hair of his head; these were they that took hold of the chain and pulled him forwards and showed him in triumph to this bloody Annas; nay these were the Judas, Jews, Annas and all; O that ever

---

[40] *The Rise of Puritanism*, p. 151; cf. L. L. Martz, *The Poetry of Meditation*, p. 163 ff.

[41] *Pace* Martz, ibid.; cf. *Grace Abounding*, para. 128; *The Greatness of the Soul, Works*, III.131. H. Talon, *John Bunyan*, p. 77.

[42] L. L. Martz, ibid., p. 163.

[43] *Workes* (1630), p. 817; cf. Baxter, *Works*, IV.286, and J. Dod, *On the Commandments*, p. 65, who says that the crucifix makes no difference between Christ and the thieves, 'but if we would see an image of Christ, looke upon poore Christians . . .'; also cf. similar sentiment in W. Perkins, *Workes*, I.755.

I should lodge within me such an heart that should lodge in it such
sins, such betrayers, such murderers of Jesus Christ.'[44]

Similarly, the nails and spear of Calvary are 'my sins'.[45]

At times, Ambrose writes with a drastic realism, as when he
points to the spectacle of the degraded yet kingly body, empurpled
in its own blood: 'Consider the piercing of his side with a spear. . . .
Methinks I see the blood running out of his side more freshly than
those golden streams which ran out of the garden of Eden.'[46]
Yet Ambrose is never so merely historical as Guevara, and while
he pleads with us for our tears at the thought of this most grievous
passion, he makes clear, in faithfulness to Scripture, that apart
from our faith that here is God's assurance of eternal life, 'the
contemplation of Christ's death would be altogether unprofitable
for us'. 'O my soul that thou wouldest thus meditate and thus
imitate, that so thy meditation might be fruitful and thy imitation
real; I mean that thy life and death might be conformable to the
life and death of Jesus Christ.'[47]

Having observed the historical events of the Passion, Ambrose
now bids us desire, hope in, believe in, love, joy, call on, and
conform to Jesus in this respect.[48] The sufferings and death of
Jesus should kindle in us ardent, burning desires. The thought of
His love and the pains to which it has carried Him should inspire
our raptures. Yet even these are insufficient 'for the admiration
of this infinite mercy'.

And now look upon him! He hangs on the cross all naked, torn, all
bloody, betwixt heaven and earth, as if he were cast out of heaven and
also rejected by earth; he has a crown indeed, but such a one as few
men will touch, none will take from him . . . his hair is all clodded with
blood, his face is clouded with black and blue; he is all over pitifully
rent, outwards, inwards, body and soul . . . I will think the rest: Alas!
when I have spoken all I can, I shall speak under it, had I the tongues
of men and of angels I could not express it. O love more deep than

---

[44] *Looking unto Jesus*, p. 274.
[45] ibid., pp. 296 ff.
[46] ibid., p. 305.
[47] ibid., pp. 305-6. For a moving modern exposition of 'Conformation' see D.
Bonhoeffer, *Ethics* (Eng. edn, 1955), pp. 17 ff.
[48] cf. the *Stimulus Amoris* probably written by James of Milan, a Friar Minor, toward
the end of the thirteenth century. The Passion, he says, may be considered for our
imitation, compassion, exultation, transformation, and repose. See Bede Frost, *The
Art of Mental Prayer*, p. 74.

hell! O love more high than heaven! The brightest seraphims that burn in love are but as sparkles to that mighty flame of love that burns in the heart of Jesus![49]

This utter sacrifice is the crowning example of what Samuel Rutherford once called 'The Drawing Loveliness of Christ'[50] Says Ambrose: 'The whole gospel is no other thing than a motive to draw man to God by the force of God's love to man'. 'O that all our words were words of love, and all our thoughts, thoughts of love, that we might speak of love, and muse of love, and love this Christ who hath first loved us, with all our heart and soul and might.'[51]

There are also many echoes in Puritan writings of Augustinian devotion to the Passion. Lewis Bayly's *The Practice of Piety* concludes with '*The Soul's Soliloquie ravished in contemplation of the Passion of our Lord*'. This is an English version of the prayer '*Quid commisisti dulcissime puer, ut sic iudicaris?*', attributed to St Augustine, and found in the writings of the eleventh-century Archbishop, St Anselm:

What hast thou done O my sweet Saviour, and aye blessed Redeemer that thou was thus betrayed of Judas, sold of the Jewes, apprehended as a malefactor, and led bound as a Lamb to the slaughter? What evil hadst thou committed that thou shouldst be thus openly arraigned, accused falsely, and unjustly condemned? What was thine offence? or to whom didst thou ever wrong? . . . What is the cause then, O Lord, of this thy cruel ignominy, Passion and death? I, O Lord, I am the cause of these thy sorrows: my sins wrought thy shame, mine iniquities are the occasion of thy injuries, I have committed the fault, and thou art plagued for the offence: I am guilty and thou art arraigned: I committed the sin and thou sufferedst the death: I have done the crime and thou hangst on the Cross. O the deepness of God's love! O the wonderful disposition of the heavenly grace! O the unmeasurable measure of the divine mercie! The wicked transgresseth and the just is punished: the guiltie is let escape and the innocent is arraigned: the malefactor is acquitted and the harmless condemned: what the evil man deserveth, the good man suffereth; the servant doth

---

[49] *Looking unto Jesus*, p. 321.

[50] *Christ Dying and Drawing Sinners to Himselfe*.

[51] op. cit. J. Wesley included Ambrose in the *Christian Library*. The hymns of Charles Wesley echo many of his sentiments, e.g.

> O that my every breath were praise!
> O that my heart were filled with God! (*MHB*, No. 452).

the fault, the master endures the strokes. What shall I say? Man sinneth and God dyeth. . . . Foolish Eve smiled when I laughed; but blessed Mary wept when thy heart bled and died. . . . Oh my Lord! . . . though I can never pay thee in that measure of love which thou hast deserved, yet I may endeavour to repay thee in such a manner as thou vouchsavest to accept in mercy.[52]

THE SACRED HEART

The seventeenth century saw the inauguration of the cult of the Sacred Heart in the Roman Church. St John Eudes in 1646 instituted the feast of the Holy Heart of Mary, and in 1672 that of the Sacred Heart of Jesus; one year later began the revelations to St Marguerite-Marie-Alacoque at Paray-le-Monial. Does this devotion owe anything to Puritan piety?[53]

Henri Bremond distinguishes between the Eudist devotion and

---

[52] op. cit., pp. 364-8; cf. P. Pourrat, *Christian Spirituality*, II.16-17, and the hymn of Samuel Crossman (1624-83), an ejected Puritan who later conformed and died Dean of Bristol.

> *O who am I*
> *That for my sake*
> *My Lord should take*
> *Frail flesh, and die?* (MHB, No. 144)

The same devotional tradition is found in the contemporary hymn of Johann Heermann (1585-1647):

> *Ah, holy Jesu, how hast Thou offended*
> *That man to judge Thee hath in hate pretended?*
> *By foes derided, by Thine own rejected,*
> *O most afflicted.*

> *Who was the guilty? Who brought this upon Thee?*
> *Alas, my treason, Jesu, hath undone Thee;*
> *'Twas I, Lord Jesu, I it was denied Thee;*
> *I crucified Thee.*

> *Lo, the good Shepherd for the sheep is offered;*
> *The slave hath sinnèd, and the Son hath suffered;*
> *For man's atonement, while he nothing heedeth,*
> *God intercedeth.*

> *For me, kind Jesu, was Thy incarnation*
> *Thy mortal sorrow, and Thy life's oblation*
> *Thy death of anguish and Thy bitter passion,*
> *For my salvation.*

> *Therefore, kind Jesu, since I cannot pay Thee,*
> *I do adore Thee, and will ever pray Thee,*
> *Think on Thy pity and Thy love unswerving,*
> *Not my deserving.* (MHB, No. 177)

[53] B. L. Manning suggests that it may. But he does not make the important distinction of Bremond (*Hymns of Watts and Wesley*, 4th edn. 1944, p. 133).

that of Paray.[54] The former is theocentric, directed to the heart
of Jesus as embodying His '*intérieur*', His heavenly priesthood and
love to the Father; the latter is directed to Christ's human heart,
yearning with love and broken with pain for men. The Paray
cult has certainly been more influential in the Roman Church,
but when the Puritans consider the Heart of Jesus, it is less as an
organ of His human Body than as His eternal disposition. It is
thus that we may interpret Ambrose above, writing of 'the mighty
flame of love that burns in the heart of Jesus'; and Richard
Baxter, saying: 'If thou know him not by the face, the voice, the
hands, if thou know him not by the tears and bloody sweat, yet
look nearer, thou mayest know him by the heart: that broken
healed heart is his: that soul pitying, melting heart is his, doubtless
it can be none's but his, love and compassion are its certain
signatures; this is he, even this is he, who would rather die than
thou shouldst die, who chooses thy life before his own, who
pleads his blood before his Father, and makes continual intercession for thee.'[55]

And certainly this is Thomas Goodwin's meaning in his
treatise on *The Heart of Christ in Heaven toward Sinners on Earth*.[56]
He begins with a commentary on the farewell discourses of the
Fourth Gospel. Christ is within sight of His glory, but His heart is
not entirely upon the saints and patriarchs to whom He is going,
nor upon His perfect fellowship with the Father; He loves His
own who are left in the world. He stoops low to wash their feet as
an earnest of the full cleansing which shall be theirs hereafter.
He promises an immediacy of communion by prayer. He will not
go alone to heaven. It is as though He says to God: 'I have thy
company, but I must have theirs too.'[57] The seventeenth chapter
of St John, says Goodwin—the Calvinist here following Arminius
—is a summary or 'platform' of Christ's intercession for us in
heaven. And so he continues, and illustrates from the Resurrection and Ascension Christ's everlasting love for sinners.

The second part of the treatise demonstrates that the heart of
the human nature of Christ continues the same for ever. His

[54] *Literary History*, III.536-72. There is a much epitomized account in a small but
most carefully annotated book by Charles Smyth, *The Friendship of Christ* (London,
1945), pp. 80 ff.

[55] *Works*, XXIII.352.

[56] *Works*, IV.93 ff.

[57] op. cit., pp. 103-4.

eternal disposition is to love sinners, for this is the Father's command. There is no conflict within the divine nature. And human love is the analogy of the divine. We behold in earthly covenants faithfully observed, the shadow of the faithfulness of God. Marriage illustrates the love of Christ for His Church. The holy love of Moses who would be blotted out for the salvation of Israel, and of Paul wishing to be anathema from Christ for the sake of his people, are types and tokens of God's love in Christ. This love inhabits Heaven's highest place. What was an Old Testament similitude is now a reality—'God might be for ever said to be compassionate as a man'.[58]

This is far removed from Nygren. It is a union of the theocentric and the anthropocentric. Christ is seen always in His relation to God. The human Jesus is the manifestation on earth of the Eternal Son of the Father. His mission is to lead men to God. But the very love of God itself is human, though it transcends by infinity all we ourselves know of love. Yet we must not despise the compassions of our hearts, lest we reject the gift of God within us.

Goodwin's treatise is also far removed from the devotions of Guevara or Ambrose. He follows Christ into Heaven to His eternal and ever-present work. He does not 'return to Golgotha and watch the sacred blood drip to the ground'.

Thus Professor Martz has good evidence besides his quotation from Baxter, for his contention that Puritan piety is more occupied with the eternal Christ than with the historical Jesus. But these two are one, and the Puritans did not divide the natures. To say that their concern was with Christ's 'official role' rather than His personality is to treat the fact that Milton was unable to complete the poem he began on the Passion as more representative of the Puritan attitude than it is, and to ignore these examples of an adoration, at once passionate and triumphant, of the Crucified and Ascended Lord.

IS THERE A PURITAN MYSTICISM?

Bernard of Clairvaux regarded devotion to the sacred humanity as the first degree of a love which should reach its climax in the love of mystical contemplation.[59] In the seventeenth century many

---

[58] op. cit., p. 139; cf. J. D. Benoît, *Calvin: Directeur d'Ames*, p. 79, for a summary of similar ideas in Calvin, and a claim that Calvin influenced the Catholic Bérulle.
[59] e.g. see Pourrat, *Christian Spirituality*, II.66 ff.

followed Bernard to his own conclusion, especially in France. Was there any manifestation of the temper of French piety among the English Puritans?

On the outskirts of the Puritan movement there were those who followed closely the teaching of Dionysius the Areopagite and the *Theologia Germanica*.[60] John Everard translated both treatises, and his disciple, Giles Randall, issued the *Theologia Germanica* in 1646. This is the summary of medieval mysticism, derived from Eckhart and Tauler, which Luther praised in his early days, and Calvin abominated. There was also a school of English mysticism derived from Jacob Boehme.[61]

Our authors, as we have seen, use the word 'mystical', and desire a relationship with Christ more immediate than any which rests on the outward knowledge of the bare facts of His life and death alone. They wrote of the Catholic 'Mistical Divines' as of those who kept alive the true spiritual religion even amid Papal darkness.[62] If (with Rufus Jones) we define mysticism as 'the type of religion which puts the emphasis on immediate awareness of relation with God, on direct and ultimate consciousness of the Divine Presence, . . . religion in its most acute and living stage',[63] it might be just possible to count the Puritans as mystics. But on a definition such as Heiler's, with its emphasis on the absorption of the personality, the Puritans are categorically outside the company of mystics. And even Rufus Jones's words would have to be revised in order to make the Puritans conform, for the Puritans' 'immediate awareness' is never—if the paradox be allowed—unmediated, and the divine Presence which they seek is that savingly revealed in Christ, and shared with His people, in the body of Christ.

The 'mystical union' of which the Puritans write is not the goal of the Christian life only, but its beginning. It may indeed be realized more by the believer as time goes on, but it is a part of justification. For the Puritan, the 'three ways' are not so much purgation, illumination, union, though these are very real elements of the Christian life, but justification, sanctification, and glorification.

[60] For an account see e.g. Inge, *Christian Mysticism*, pp. 181 ff.
[61] See Nils Thune, *The Behemenists and the Philadelphians, a Contribution to the Study of English Mysticism in the Seventeenth and Eighteenth Centuries* (Uppsala, 1948).
[62] e.g. T. Goodwin and P. Nye, Introduction to T. Hooker's *Application of Redemption*.
[63] *Studies in Mystical Religion*, p. xv (London, 1909).

Thus, when the Puritans borrow from Catholic or mystical writers, they make the expressions serve the purpose of their own evangelical piety. The Song of Songs was in the Puritans' Bible and they could not divorce themselves from the long tradition of Christian commentary upon it.[64] But when Richard Sibbes expounds it, the Bride is primarily the Church, though since 'all Christian favours belong to all Christians alike ... every Christian soule is the Spouse of Christ as well as the whole Church'.[65] The kisses of the divine Lover's mouth are Christ's presence in the ordinances; the Sacraments are His love tokens; and though the soul longs for Christ most ardently and every taste whets her appetite the more, she receives Him in His appointed ways and not, as a rule, through special and private raptures. This desire for Christ is manifested outwardly and ethically. It implies a love of doing His will in good words.[66]

Francis Rous (1579-1659), a Cornish layman, who in the course of his long career was Provost of Eton and Speaker of the Commons, and, ecclesiastically, passed from the Presbyterians to the Independents, wrote a treatise on *The Mysticall Marriage*. He is much influenced by Canticles, and writes in the knowledge of mystical terms and ways of thought, but there is no doubt of his evangelical foundation. For him, mystical union is a kind of intermediate state between sinful historical existence and the pure life of the Godhead, but the union is mediated by Christ. The soul is too unclean to touch God 'in immediate unity; but there is a pure counterpart of thy nature, and that pure humanity is immediately knit to the purest Deity'.[67] Jesus Christ is one with God by personal union; the human soul can be made one with God by 'mystical union'.

Rous also sees the mystical marriage itself as an eschatological event. The full consummation must wait until after death, but Christ, and the loving, believing soul are even now in that betrothal which, as we have seen from Puritan social custom, was a solemn marriage contract.[68] This means as the inevitable precondition that the old husband—the old self—must be slain.

The possession of Christ is a universe within itself. He 'is all

---

[64] For an account of this see W. R. Inge, *Christian Mysticism*, App. D.
[65] *The Spouse* (London, 1638), pp. 13-14.
[66] ibid., pp. 22, 29-30, 51-2, 53-4.
[67] op. cit., pp. 8-9.
[68] *The Mysticall Marriage*, p. 43.

lights in one light, all glories in one glorie, all beauties in one beauty, all joyes in one joy'.[69] United with Christ, the soul 'hath him by whom the worlds were made, and therefore she hath all the worlds made by him'.[70] One is reminded of a saying of Kagawa's about the physical universe: 'God threw it all in when he gave me Christ.'[71] Like St Bernard, Rous insists that contemplation must be joined with activity. 'Obedience is the kindly fruite of a loving soule, and a loving soule bringeth forth this fruite as kindly as a good tree bringeth forth good fruite.'[72] He rebukes those contemplatives who would separate mystical divinity from practical. 'Too much enjoying is a losse of enjoying; for it loseth all those gaines annexed to doing and suffering.'[73] Perhaps he is oversanguine about the power of persecution to strengthen love; yet few of those who know what the love of God means would deny that 'there is a peculiar height and abundance of consolations, which none can attain unto, but those that have a special height and abundance of tribulations'.[74]

Rous knows that in this life the divine Lover at times withdraws the consolation of His presence, and this is why 'His best coming is his last coming . . . without any more going asunder'.[75] Rous is not unaware of the 'dark night' which St John of the Cross describes. There are 'ugly shapes in the dark night of desertions', as Christian knew in the dark valley of *Pilgrim's Progress*. Old lusts storm the soul and would defile her purity. But even these desertions are part of the purpose of divine love. They will be seen to have worked great good when the day breaks and shadows flee away. 'When he comes againe thou wilt hold him faster, and keepe him surer, and so enjoy him nearer and longer.'[76] The soul must learn that she cannot both entertain Christ's enemies and keep Him; neither can pride make a bed for the Beloved. Moreover, our love should be strengthened by trials; this way alone can it transcend feeling. How easily we confuse emotional pleasures, feelings of assurance, with the true love of Christ! What a low degree of love it is that dies when Christ is hidden from the soul, or that will not understand when He rebukes her sin! Christ and His love 'are thine when thou seest or feelest not that they are thine. . . . He and his love are better than the seeing and feeling

---

[69] *The Mysticall Marriage*, pp. 44-5.   [70] ibid., p. 56.
[71] Quoted E. C. Blackman, *Marcion* (London, 1948), p. 32.   [72] op. cit., p. 73.
[73] ibid., p. 84.   [74] ibid., p. 79.   [75] *The Mysticall Marriage*, pp. 93-4.   [76] ibid., p. 113.

of him and his love; . . . better for thee that they are thine, than that they appear to be thine; . . . therefore at all times and in all estates, even in darkest desertions and greatest sufferings, trust him whose love turns all things to good unto his beloved, even death unto life'. The Bridegroom is the Christ who suffered for all mankind, and broke the gates and bars of death that we might enter the life eternal.[77]

So in the Beloved's absence the soul must 'sigh and pray and read and hear', ejaculating amid earthly labours, preparing herself 'as a bride that looks for her husband'. She may have to be content with these 'lower' works, but all the while she can fix her mind on the place where joys are incessant. In this life the soul is 'lodged in a house of clay, and the traffic between her and her husband is but by some chink which the spirit hath bored', but there, *in patria*, is uninterrupted felicity with 'nothing between'.

Rous, however, is more concerned with the visitations which the soul's husband does vouchsafe. Then is the time to 'lay up a stocke of confidence and comfort for times of scarcitie'.[78] The soul always stands over against Christ; she is not mystically absorbed in Him. The relationship, in Deissmann's phrase, is *com*-union rather than union. Rous's signs of a true visitation are biblical and ethical. The divine Visitor is the Christ who speaks by His redeeming acts in history. Light, joy, and holiness accompany Him. Human reason is not annihilated. 'The reasonable light of man continueth in man, even when this supernaturall light shineth, it knows what other men know, and knows that itselfe knewe and thought before this light came to it; but this light being come, it yeelds willingly to it, and surrenders both itself and the man whom it formerly guided.'[79] Thus the author does not follow the procession of mystics along the *via negativa*. Union with Christ is ethical. It is conformity of will. The more Christ comes into a soul by His Spirit, 'the more spiritual he doth make her; yea the more he doth melt a soule in himselfe; the more he doth turne her will into his will, and the more doth he increase

---

[77] *The Mysticall Marriage*, pp. 144 ff; cf. H. Scougal, *The Life of God in the Soul of Man*, p. 114, for similar deprecation of mere feelings.

[78] ibid., pp. 202-3; cf. R. Bolton, *Preparation before Death*, p. 30, Ignatius Loyola, *Spiritual Exercises*, p. 188: 'Let him who is in consolation think how it will be with him in the desolation that will follow, laying up fresh strength for that time.'

[79] ibid., p. 239.

descriptions of Christ's sufferings from unhealthy sentimentalism. But it is not the language of absorption.

Is there then a Puritan mysticism? We have discovered an intense desire for immediacy of communion with God, though this is always understood as possible only in Christ. The adjective 'mystical' is used, though in a sense derived from Scripture, and with its neo-Platonist associations subordinate.[92] There is no mysticism of absorption or of the 'inner light'. The union with Christ for which the Puritans longed is available for all who are justified believers. It is no short cut to Heaven which dispenses with the fellowship of the Church and Sacraments. And it awaits its perfect consummation in the Kingdom of God.[93]

Yet the Puritans did not ignore the inheritance of Catholic spirituality. They understood the heights and depths, the light and darkness of spiritual religion. They knew that the dark night of the soul is no mere fantasy of mystical mania, but an experience which the most mature Christians may be called upon to share with the Lord Christ. 'The Sonne of God himself knew dereliction', writes Paul Baynes.[94] In this world there must at times be doubt and tribulation; the believer himself will sometimes turn to sin; but the passionate yearning for Christ is a yearning also for Heaven, where He is all in all, and clouds and darkness are fled away, and obedience is perfected.

---

[92] See Chapter 3, *supra*.

[93] *S.J.T.*, VIII.III.315 ff: a review of Lief Eeg-Olofsson, *The Conception of the Inner Light in Robert Barclay's Theology*. For Calvin's mysticism see J. D. Benoît, *Calvin: Directeur d'Ames* (Strasbourg, 1944), pp. 76 ff.

[94] *Christian Letters*, unpaginated; cf. the following story from *The Worthy Sayings of Old Mr Dod*, p. 15: 'A goodly Minister being in a Consumption came to Ashby not far from Fawely to have the help of Mr Dod's counsels and comforts. He was much oppressed with melancholy, and a little before his Death asked Mr Dod: 'What will you say to me, that am going out of the world, and can find no Comfort?' To whom he said: "What will you say of our Saviour, who, when he was going out of the World, found no comfort but cried out, 'My God, my God, why hast thou forsaken me?'"' This speech much refreshed the Minister a little before he went to his heavenly Inheritance.' It seems probable that the Minister was John Preston.

Of all Divinity that part is most useful which determines Cases of Conscience.

JOSEPH HALL

When we came to the Hill Difficulty, he made no stick at that, nor did he much fear the lions: for you must know that his trouble was not about such things as those: his fear was about his acceptance at the last.

JOHN BUNYAN

CHAPTER SEVEN

EVANGELICAL SCHOLASTICISM

THE PASTORAL OFFICE

'THE Lord', writes Richard Greenham, 'hath given unto the Ministers of his Gospel the power of binding and loosing both in the public ministry of his word, and also in the private consolation of his children.'[1] We may venture to dispute Haller's assertion that the diary was the Puritan substitute for the confessional.[2] The Puritans, like Calvin, abolished the grille, and supplanted what they deemed a tyrannous pseudo-sacramental superstition by the godly counsel of learned divines, but they regarded the minister as above all else a spiritual director; if not the 'lord of faith', the 'helper of joy'.[3]

We have many examples of the way in which the Puritans exercised the spiritual ministry. 'Every Thursday evening', says Baxter, 'my neighbours that were most desirous and had opportunity, met at my House, and there one of them repeated the Sermon; and afterwards they proposed what Doubts any of them had about the Sermon, or any other Case of Conscience, and I resolved their Doubts.'[4] Often the counsel was more private. Some rules, which Richard Greenham once sent to a gentlewoman troubled in mind, are reprinted in *A Garden of Spirituall Flowers*, and include this plea: 'Oh pardon me if I be bold in this one thing. I trust I rejoice more in the good of your soule than ever I should rejoice in the fruit of mine own body. It would be a thousand deaths, yea a thousand hels unto me to see your soule miscarrie. Oh let me be accepted more than a civill friend, more than a friend of the world. Give me this benefit to be thought farther than a friend of the flesh.' Baxter is not unwilling to grant absolution a kind of sacramental authority,[5]

---

[1] *A Letter Consolatorie, Works* (1605 edn).
[2] *Rise of Puritanism*, p. 38.
[3] cf. Calvin, *Inst.*, III.4; J. D. Benoît, *Calvin: Directeur d'Ames*. J. Owen, *Works*, IV.123.
[4] *Reliquiae Baxterianae*, I.83.
[5] *Works*, XIV.449 f.

and he never tires of insisting that for the very life of their souls, believers must follow such preachers as are 'judicious, faithful, serious, searching, powerful'.[6] Like Greenham, he compares ministers with physicians:

And Ministers are not set up only for public preaching, but for private counsel also, according to our particular needs. As physicians are not only to read you instructions for the dieting and curing of yourselves; but to be present in your sickness, to direct you in the particular application of remedies. And as lawyers are to assist you in your particular cases to free your estates from encumbrances, and to preserve or rescue them from contentious men. Choose therefore some able Minister to be your ordinary counsellor in the matters of God. And let him be one that is humble, faithful, experienced, and skilful; that hath leisure, ability, and willingness to assist you.[7]

With this counsellor, our dealings must be the frankest possible. He is not infallible, but his judgements must be well heeded. The Puritans did not think in terms of a few gifted directors of a few fastidious penitents. Robert Bolton declares their aim:

Every faithful Minister is to every Christian under his charge, and within the exercise and enjoyment of his ministry, either a spirituall Father or a spirituall Tutor; a blessed Instrument unto him either of plantation or preservation of grace, either of the first happy inspiration, or the after comfortable continuance of spiritual life; either he hath begot him unto God by the immortall seed, or brings him up in the trade of godlinesse by the sincere milk of the Word.[8]

Reproof was among the duties of the minister. In one of Paul Baynes's letters a noble lady is taken to task. One of the signs of her fall from grace is that she has dispensed with the 'constant residence of one who might be a private seer to you'. A frequent change of preachers is as bad for the soul as a weekly change of nurses for a baby, not least because a strange minister cannot admonish! But the pastors will be more often sons of consolation than of thunder; they will be tender, self-abasing, not over-austere, 'ready to shew that mercy they have felt before themselves'. 'There be many broken spirits need soft and oily words. The mission of the pastor is that of Him whose life is prefigured by

[6] *Works*, II.113 ff.   [7] ibid., pp. 116-17.   [8] *A Discourse of True Happinesse*, p. 199.

the servant of the Lord: 'A bruised reed shall he not break, and smoking flax shall he not quench.'[9]

PURITAN CASUISTRY

When we come to investigate the sources of Puritan pastoral theology, we are confronted by one of the greatest problems of the post-Reformation period. The Reformers themselves broke free of what they believed were the shackles of scholasticism. They renounced the medieval logic of conscience with its many fine distinctions, such as that between mortal and venial sin. Such laborious reasoning seemed to Luther and Calvin to lead into a futile and hopeless maze of self-justification. It is therefore with some surprise that we find almost at the beginning of Perkins's *Cases of Conscience* a thorough examination 'of the nature and difference of sinne', in which he asserts strongly that all sins are not equal, and declares: 'Now though every sinne of it selfe be mortall, yet all are not equally mortall; but some more, some lesse.'[10] Baxter is quite open that to distinguish between mortal and venial sin is 'of very great necessity'.[11]

The Puritans unblushingly follow Catholic casuists. There is an engaging account of John Preston reading Aquinas at the barber's:[12] 'If hair fell on the page he blew it off and read on.' (We are tempted to comment in Sam Weller's words: 'That's philosophy, sir, ain't it?') William Ames quotes whole passages from William of Paris and is not ashamed to consider himself his namesake's retailer in his own generation.[13] He also answers questions according to traditional Catholic judgement; for instance, to the dilemma, 'When a man doth apprehend that of two sins he must needs commit one, which is he to choose?' he

---

[9] R. Sibbes, *Works*, I.53 ff. It must be remembered that the extremer Puritans did not always commit discipline to the Minister alone, and that the Protestant casuists of the seventeenth century as a whole wrote for masters of families and private Christians as well as to help Pastors in their duties. John Robinson has a letter suggesting that for direction as distinct from routine government a special committee of a few elders be set up. See H. M. Dexter, *The Congregationalists of the Last Three Hundred Years*, esp. pp. 450-1 for this and other examples; cf. F. J. Powicke, *Henry Barrow*, etc. (London, 1900), pp. 104-5.

[10] *Workes*, II.9.

[11] *Works*, III.336 ff.

[12] Quoted W. Haller, *Rise of Puritanism*, p. 142.

[13] The Appendix to Ames's second book of *Conscience with the Power and the Cases Thereof* consists of 33 theses on Temptations, drawn from William of Paris; and there are several other references beside, e.g. Book I.24, and a prayer of Confession, Book V.135.

answers in the usual Thomist manner: 'He sins lesse which commits the lesser sin.'[14]

Ames recognizes that it is pastoral extremity which has made Protestants thus dependent on 'Popish authors'. Like Thomas Fuller and Jeremy Taylor, he uses the example of the Israelites going down to the Philistines to sharpen 'every man his share, his Mattocke, or his Axe or his weeding Hooke'.[15] Nor is this a phenomenon solely of British Protestantism in the seventeenth century. The student of Heinrich Heppe's *Reformed Dogmatics*[16] discovers that the teaching of Calvin is wedded somewhat uneasily to the logic of the Schoolmen in more than one contemporary theologian of Switzerland, Holland and Germany. At this stage the whole of Protestantism seems to have been concentrated in Church discipline and practical divinity. And the Puritans found it urgently necessary to frame a method to guide wayfaring pilgrims.

But they were not wilfully betraying the Reformation or disregarding the Scriptures. They believed, as Ames says, that there were some veins of silver among the 'earth and dirt' of Roman superstitions. They did not extend the same hospitality to their Jesuit contemporaries as to their medieval predecessors. Edmund Bunny's notorious adaptation of a manual by the Jesuit Parsons was not of a work which contained the Society's later moral theology.[17] The historian of the Jesuits, Father James Brodrick, has lamented the 'speculative laxity' of some of their casuists.[18] And above this there was a vital difference of principle between the Jesuit and Protestant conception of moral theology. For the former it tended too often to be a calculation of the minimum required to keep the Commandments; for the latter it was the 'Divine Science' of holy living, and its aim was the growth of the Christian character in the grace of Christ.[19] It was nothing less

[14] ibid., Book III.87; cf. K. E. Kirk, *Some Principles of Moral Theology*, p. 200.

[15] 1 Samuel, 13[20]. *Conscience with the Power and the Cases Thereof:* 'To the Reader.'

[16] 'Set out and illustrated from the Sources, originally published in German, 1861' (E.T., G. T. Thomson, 1950).

[17] *A Book of Christian Exercises pertaining to Resolution* (1582). Parson's manual was derived from Gaspar Loarte.

[18] *The Economic Morals of the Jesuits* (London, 1934), pp. 24-5, quoted T. Wood, *English Casuistical Divinity*, p. 63.

[19] cf. T. Wood, ibid., p. 64. Wood's excellent book shows that in this branch of theology the Puritans and the casuists of the 'High Church' school were at one. In this, his book is to be preferred to H. R. McAdoo, *The Structure of Caroline Moral Theology*, who tries to distinguish between Puritans and Anglicans but cannot keep the distinction clear.

than the attempt to relate the Christian Gospel to the whole of life. And as we shall see, there was one branch of Puritan casuistry which was unique.

CONSCIENCE AND ITS CASES

The Puritans place conscience in the understanding. It is not 'moral sense' but 'practical reason'. 'There is no trace in Caroline theology, nor for that matter among the Reformed moralists, of that view of conscience as seated in the conative side of our nature which has been identified with the Franciscan Schoolmen. Everywhere, the Thomist view prevails.'[20] Perkins regards it as a faculty, a 'created quality', 'from which knowledge and judgement proceed as effects. . . . Every particular man hath his own particular conscience' which 'alone of the faculties of the mind determines things done'. Conscience is set between man and God, making them 'partners in the knowledge of one and the same secret'.[21] Ames, following Aquinas in particular, defines conscience as 'a man's judgment of himself according to the judgment of God of him', where 'judgment' means 'an act of practical judgment, proceeding from the understanding by the power or means of a Habit'.[22]

The Puritans revive the old scholastic syllogism of conscience. The word translated 'conscience' in the New Testament is '*syneidesis*', but this was referred to the minor premise of the syllogism, to the personal application of the truth of the major, which was called the '*synteresis*'. The original meaning of this word is not known. Jerome describes it as the '*scintilla conscientiae*' remaining in Cain 'after he was expelled from paradise'.[23] Ames says that it is a habit of the understanding by which we give assent to the principles of moral actions, since 'through the goodness of God the knowledge of many things which we ought to do or shun are still conserved in man's mind even after his fall'.[24] Ames chooses as an example of *synteresis* this proposition: 'He that lives in sin shall die.' The *syneidesis* would then give: 'I live in sin'; and the conclusion or crisis would then be: 'Therefore I

---

[20] H. R. McAdoo, ibid., p. 66.

[21] *A Discourse of Conscience, Workes* (1605 edn), pp. 619 ff.

[22] *Conscience*, Book I.2, 3; cf. Aquinas, *Summa Theol.*, Part I, Q.79.12.

[23] K. E. Kirk, *Some Principles of Moral Theology*, p. 178.

[24] *Conscience*, p. 4; cf. Aquinas, *Summa Theol.*, I-II, Q94, aI, ad.2.

die.' The full working of conscience must always include this act of judgement, and pastors must see that men bring their reasoning to conclusion, for in trying to escape judgement men also escape salvation.

Luther had broken with the doctrine of *synteresis*. The references to conscience in his *Letters of Spiritual Counsel* are conventional— he talks of a good conscience, and the supremacy of conscience over external authority—but the account of his struggles would suggest that, in his own experience, conscience was essentially *syneidesis* and a tormentor who could only be silenced by faith in him who justifies the ungodly.[25] An erudite and exhaustive modern study of *Conscience in the New Testament* supports this aspect of evangelical experience that conscience is something from which we need to be delivered.[26] *Syneidesis*, says Mr Pierce, is the 'painful reaction of man's nature, as morally responsible against infringements of its created limits—past, present by virtue of initiation in the past, habitual or characteristic by virtue of past infringements'.[27] It may be described as the voice of God. But it warns against transgressions; it does not give infallible guidance.

The Puritans regarded *synteresis* as scriptural, the apprehension of the law of nature. No man is so depraved as to be utterly void of it.[28] For the Christian, natural law is enlightened by the Scriptures. The Puritans may have given to *synteresis* a more positive function than the Bible, examined by modern scholarship, would warrant, but their ultimate fidelity to the word of God saved them from that popular idolatry of conscience which Mr Pierce exposes so vigorously. Baxter limits the authority of conscience: it 'is not appointed or authorised to make us any duty which God hath not made us; but only to discern the law of God, and call upon us to observe it: and an erring conscience is not to be obeyed, but to be better informed and brought to a righter performance of its office.'[29] And the whole aim of Puritan casuistry was that men might not be left to the vagaries and perils

[25] See Luther's *Letters of Spiritual Counsel* (ed. Tappert, London, 1955), pp. 68, 83, 98, 110, 123, 224; G. Rupp, *Luther's Progress to the Diet of Worms* (London, 1951), pp. 26-47.
[26] C. A. Pierce (London, 1955).
[27] ibid., p. 108.
[28] e.g. Romans 2[15]. Ames also finds an appeal to natural conscience in I Corinthians 6[9], and enlightened conscience in Romans 6[3]. An example of *synteresis* would also be I Corinthians 11[14]: 'Does not nature itself teach you that for a man to wear long hair is degrading to himself, but if a woman has long hair it is her pride?'
[29] *Works*, II.336-7.

of private judgement, but given through the Church the help they could not find alone. And they believed that the blood of Christ confutes the major or minor of the syllogism and invalidates the dread conclusion.

Perkins, Ames and Baxter are the most outstanding and exhaustive of the Puritans in their resolution of cases of conscience. The task leads them to discuss every aspect of Christian belief and behaviour from the fear of God to the preparation of sermons. Hardly any question of Christian morality or any problem of pastoral guidance escapes them. We can best understand their methods by looking at certain types of case.

Perkins has an admirably lucid division of cases, which the others follow: 'Some concerning man simply considered by himselfe: some againe, as he stands in relation to another.'[30] The latter are subdivided into those which concern his relation to God and those which concern his relation to man, that is 'as hee is a member of one of the three societies; that is either of the Family, or of the Church, or of the Common-wealth'. We shall consider examples of some of these, but we shall defer the questions about the state of man to another section, because it is here in fact that we reach both the climax of Puritan casuistry and its distinctive contribution.

(1) *Questions about man in his relation to God*

There is much teaching about prayer, worship and the sacraments, some of which we have already considered. Ames writes with resolute common sense about scruples. The Kingdom of Heaven must often be captured by dealing violently with scruples. The attempt to remove a scruple with reason will often increase it. Evil thoughts at prayer must not be dealt with one by one, but violently ignored in a furious activity of calling upon God. 'If there be any man that is so molested through the consideration of his own unworthiness that he dare scarce be so bold as to come to the Lord's Table though he find in himselfe true faith and Repentance; he may and ought, not withstanding this scruple, come to the Lord's Supper.'[31]

A problem which exercised many people in the years after the Reformation was that of the right attitude toward worship of

[30] *Workes*, II.12.   [31] *Conscience*, Book I.11.

which their conscience could not approve, either because the officiant was 'some country tippler mumbling a prayer between visits to the ale house',[32] or because the ceremonial seemed contrary to Scripture. Ames cannot give any certain and general rule in the matter, but he does suggest that its resolution depends on the precise sin which conscience is condemning—involvement with another's evil, or idolatry. 'It is a greater sin to neglect God's Service than to communicate with another's personall wickedness in that Service', but 'the sinne of Idolatry is greater than a neglect of true worship. In the first instance he sins more that follows his conscience than he that doth against it; but in this his sinne is greater that doth contrary to it.'[33]

(2) *Questions about man in his relation to other men*

(a) *Anger—when is it a virtue and when a vice?*

Perkins enumerates the conditions of just and lawful anger.[34] It must have a right beginning, and be inflamed, as in the Old Testament patriarchs, by an offence against God; it must be counselled and deliberate, not rash or hasty; it must be inspired by love of God and hatred of evil. Also 'we must put a difference between the *person*, and the offence or sinne of the person. The sinne of the person is the proper object of anger, and not the person but only by reason of the sin. . . . We must put a difference between the cause and offence of God, and the cause and offence of man.' Finally there is a right way of being angry. In wrath we must remember mercy. 'Anger against an offence must be mixed with sorrow for the same offence.' It must always be moderated by the claims of social duty, and must not make us refuse the reverence that we owe to parents or rulers. Unjust anger is the reverse of just—it is hasty, easily provoked, immoderate. It makes us forget our duty to God and our neighbour, and it is wholly selfish.

Perkins reveals the positive side of Puritan casuistry when he goes on to consider the remedies of unjust anger. These he divides into two—those of Meditation, and those of Practice. Under the former we are to reflect that God forbids rash and unjust anger and that He turns injuries to our good. We are to

---

[32] The phrase is Alan Simpson's, *Puritanism in Old and New England*, p. 12.
[33] *Conscience*, Book I.11.   [34] *Workes*, II.121 ff.

think of His infinite patience even with the wicked and His constant forgiveness of our own innumerable sins. Vengeance belongs to God alone, and we must learn to suffer our small wrongs in the remembrance of what Christ has suffered for us. We are also to consider that the neighbour with whom we are angry is our brother, and that we are to forgive as we ourselves hope to be forgiven. We must also think of ourselves. Rash anger subjects us to the wrath of God. We are commanded to love one another as Christ has loved us; and we ought to make allowance for circumstances in censuring others. Rash anger does not fit us for the service of God—it is injurious to body and soul alike, and it is the result, not just of physical distempers, but of a lack of reason and judgement in the mind and evil affections in the heart.

The practical remedies which Perkins proposes are five. Anger should be concealed both in word and deed. 'We must depart from them with whom we are angrie' and avoid contentions and contentious persons. We must turn our anger against ourselves, for we sin against God every day. And 'we must accustome our-selves to the daily exercises of invocation of the name of God, for this end, that hee in mercy would mortifie all our earthly affec-tions, especially this corrupt and violent affection or unjust wrath'.

This counsel is not dissimilar from what we find in Robert Bolton's *Directions for a Comfortable Walking with God.* On the 'mentall drunkennes' of ungovernable anger he recommends both a philosophic discipline and the peculiar restraints of Christian religion. We must cultivate reason, learn to put ourselves in the place of those who annoy us, to ignore petty provocations, and disregard tale-bearers. We must muzzle our curiosity about other's opinion of us, subdue our covetousness ('the cut-throat of Grace'), and overcome that horrible conceit which imagines that every whispered comment and *sotto voce* joke is against us. If choler rises we should keep still and silent ('The stirring and agitation of thy body, by stamping or slinging about, inflames the bloud and humours and the walking of thy tongue keepes both the passionate heate in thine owne heart, and many times sets on fire those that thou art angry with'), 'give reason leave to inter-pose and resolve' (by a simple device like saying over the alpha-bet!), and reflect on the 'brutish deformities' of rage and the 'sweete lovelinesse and amiable acceptation of a mild, un-passionate spirit'. These are moral precepts, counsels of natural philosophy. The Christian will add to them the recollection that all his wrongs are ordained by God for his everlasting good. 'I was dumbe I opened not my mouth because thou didst it.'[35] The wonderful patience of God with sinners who crucify afresh His Son throughout the ages, and His merciful dealings with our own criminal souls should be our final restraint. 'If hee out of the riches of his mercy hath remitted unto thee ten thousand talents, what a base wretchednesse it were to flye in the face of thy fellow servant and take him by the throat for an hundred pence.'[36]

(b) Truth and falsehood

William Ames is at his best in discussing lies.[37] He has no doubt that a lie is 'a sin abominable to God'. It disorders the self, since it sets the speech against the mind and deceives our neighbour to whom by natural law we owe the truth. 'It doth in a speciall manner hurt the Majesty of God, who is the authour, and such a lover of truth that he cannot lye: and also hath imprinted in man the image of his truth to bee kept; neither did hee ever give authority of lying by any dispensation.' Even profligates recognize something particularly base about a lie. And that which violates even such honour as there is among thieves undermines the whole structure of lawful society.

Ames does not go to the absurd lengths of Kant, who, it will be remembered, once said that he would be obliged to tell the truth even to a criminal who was looking for a friend hiding in his house. He recognizes that sometimes it is necessary to conceal the truth, even as Christ did in His silence before Pilate. He claims that this can be done without the guilt of a lie. But he repudiates all idea of 'mental reservation'; he enjoys exposing those Roman exegetes who claim to find it even in the Gospels, and delights in setting the Roman casuists against each other.

Pertinent as he is, we may find that Ames here is not quite Evangelical enough. He does not break through the formal categories of his discussion. In his unfinished *Ethics*,[38] Dietrich Bonhoeffer goes deeper. 'The lie is a contradiction of the word of God, which God has spoken in Christ, and upon which creation is

---

[35] Psalm 39[9].
[37] *Conscience*, Book V.269 ff.

[36] op. cit., pp. 95-103.
[38] London (1955), p. 332.

founded. Consequently the lie is the denial, the negation and the conscious and deliberate destruction of the reality which is created by God and which consists in God, no matter whether this purpose is achieved by speech or by silence.'

(c) The right use of money

The Puritans evolved a casuistry of economic conduct, which, as far as usury was concerned, had come to terms with the exigencies of commerce and was—unlike the medieval masters—prepared to admit that the charging of interest was not unlawful provided due forbearance and charity were exercised and greed restrained.[39] William Perkins develops his teaching about riches characteristically by propounding four rules:[40]

(1) A man is accountable to God for everything he possesses, for He is the rightful Lord of all. This is implicit in the prayer for daily bread.

(2) The rich man must if necessary be prepared to abandon all for Christ, and to possess his wealth as though he possessed it not.

(3) At the call of God riches must be forsaken. This call is given sometimes, as in the case of the Apostles, for the spreading of the Gospel, sometimes under persecution, sometimes when it is necessary for Christians to relieve the distresses of their suffering brethren. But evangelical perfection does not necessarily demand it.

(4) 'We must so use and possesse the goods we have, that the use and possession of them may tend to God's glory and the salvation of our souls.'

The Puritans condemned gaming on the grounds that a mortal man is not the absolute lord of his money. It ultimately belongs to God, and the individual has no right to hazard it, except in obedience to the command of the Gospel. Public lotteries to raise money for pious purposes are not wholly unlawful, but as usually ordered they stimulate the lust of gain, and 'give occasion to many evils'.[41]

---

[39] e.g. W. Ames, *Conscience*, Book V.239 ff. See T. Wood, *English Casuistical Divinity*, pp. 92 ff, for an admirable summary of Christian economic teaching in the seventeenth century, and the cautious attitude of the moralists to 'Occult compensation' in which the Puritans' position is virtually that of St Antonino of Florence (1389-1459). It is much too superficial to regard the Puritan attitude to wealth as altogether influenced by the precedent of the O.T. Patriarchs.

[40] *Workes*, II.126 ff.

[41] cf. W. Ames, *Conscience*, Book V.216 ff.

(d) The right use of leisure

The bow cannot always be bent, says Perkins, and therefore recreation is a necessity.[42] But it should only be in the use of things indifferent. This is why Perkins and Ames object to religious pageants and plays.[43] Nor should recreation be made of the sins of men; thus ordinary plays which set forth the misdemeanours and vices of men are altogether wrong. Before we condemn this as altogether intolerable and 'Puritanical' in the bad sense, we should at least remember the problem that confronts every minister when he has to consider the deletion of swear words in the Church Drama Group's play. To transfer evil from real life to art does display it in a new medium. It is not a valid argument to say that the blasphemy or obscenity of a drama faithfully represents 'real life'. Even so we may deplore the Puritans' blindness to the artistic values and the numinous quality of the drama, and may feel that at times their view of sin was as lacking in evangelical depth as their view of truth. Some of them at any rate were not so censorious.

It is good to be able to refute Macaulay from Perkins, who objects to bear-baiting and cock-fights because they are cruel. We should not take pleasure in 'nature red in tooth and claw'. St Francis of Sales has doubts similar to those of Perkins concerning dancing and card games.[44] Perkins allows games of wit and industry: 'Of the sort are Shooting in the long bow, Shooting in the Caleever, Running, Wrastling, Fencing, Musicke, the game of Chesse, and Draughts, the Philosophers game, and such like.' But Perkins is writing of these things under the virtue of Temperance, and he knows how easily a legitimately recreative pastime can become a distracting and devouring passion.

(e) The dissolution of marriage

William Ames's discussion of divorce is somewhat prosaic.[45] He follows conventional Protestant doctrine in regarding adultery as the sole ground of divorce, and then somewhat cautiously adds that divorce in this case is a privilege, not a precept, and no man is forbidden to forgive the offence 'so it bee without scandal'. But there are two points of special interest. First, here as elsewhere,

---

[42] *Workes*, II.140.   [43] cf. Ames, *Conscience*, Book V.216 ff.
[44] cf. *Introduction*, p. 222.   [45] *Conscience*, Book V.209-10.

Ames quotes Cajetan,[46] this time his comment on Matthew 19[9]: 'I understand therefore that it is lawfull by the law of our Lord Jesus Christ, for a Christian to put away his Wife for carnall fornication, and that hee may marry another.' Secondly, there is no doubt that the Puritan refusal to regard marriage as a sacramental bond, made indissoluble by priestly mediation, led directly to such views of divorce as Milton expresses in his tracts. Professor William Haller summarizes them thus: 'There can be no marriage without the marriage of true minds. Any other union is sin, and any law which could counsel men to sin is not law but tyranny.'[47] This exalted view leads to an argument for divorce which, though it is not to be ignored by the Christian, can be most easily abused. The true wisdom of marriage would seem to lie somewhere between Miltonic idealism and Lutheran realism, between the hope that marriage may be as the companionship of our first parents in Paradise and the experience that often it is all too much tainted by the fall, and must be safeguarded by the constraint of obligation, when romantic love has passed. The ultra-rigorist attitude toward divorce would seem to make Christ a second Moses.

(f) The Christian attitude to war

The battles of the Old Testament and the Apocalypse and the dealings both of the Baptist and the Christ with soldiers seem to the Puritans to imply that the Scripture sanctions war. Matthew 5 raises difficulties, but these sayings were believed to restrain private vengeance rather than public authority, which elsewhere (Romans 13) is said to bear the sword as from God. A just war, however, must be waged in a just cause on behalf of a just authority, and out of a zeal for justice. Ames says any commonwealth has the right to defend itself but only a perfect commonwealth can legitimately wage an aggressive war.[48] Moreover, as moral theologians have always insisted, its methods of war must not transgress the laws of nature and of God; as far as possible it should be fought only against offenders, not against civil populations. Thus Ames stands in the tradition of those who, from the

---

[46] Thomas de Vio Cardinal Cajetan (1469-1534) was the legate sent to interview Luther at Augsburg in 1518. He became an Erasmian and would have been condemned as a heretic had he lived a few days longer.

[47] *Liberty and Reformation*, p. 95.

[48] *Conscience*, Book V.184 ff.

K

Mosaic law onward, have sought to restrain the barbarities of group action and civilize the jungle of human relationships. The problems of the present day are more complicated, but it may be doubted whether the world has yet learned these elementary principles of the old moral theology, or whether contemporary ecclesiastical pronouncements go much beyond them.

Richard Baxter also deals with this subject, and his judgement too is in line with traditional moral theology. Christian Kings and States, he says, are as much as individuals bound to love their enemies. 'Therefore they must raise no war unnecessarily, nor for any cause be it never so just in itself, when the benefits of the war are not likely to be a greater good than the war will bring hurt, both to friends and foes set together. A lawful offensive war is almost like a true general council; on certain suppositions such a thing may be; but whether the world ever saw such a thing, or whether such suppositions will come to existence, is the question.'[49]

THE GREATEST CASE OF ALL

There is, however, another, graver question for the casuist. William Perkins asks it in his memorable title: *A Case of Conscience the Greatest that ever was; how a man may know whether he be the child of God or no.*'[50] Here is the distinctively Puritan and evangelical contribution. What to Perkins was the greatest conceivable case of conscience is relegated to the treatment of eccentric scruples in most Catholic manuals—if indeed it receives mention at all.[51] Many writers regard the desire for assurance as a dangerous mental aberration, responsible for the worst excesses of the narrowest Puritanism.[52] The Council of Trent repudiated the search for assurance: 'No man can know with certainty of faith which cannot be subject to error, that he has obtained the grace of God.'

Is it so eccentric to want to know our standing with God? We are for ever revolving our own thoughts about God, and we can be obsessed with other people's opinions of us. Is it altogether misguided to want to know what God thinks about us? Can there

---

[49] *Works*, VI.472.

[50] The Treatise is I John arranged as a dialogue between John and the Church.

[51] e.g. H. Davis, S.J., *Moral and Pastoral Theology* (London, 1935), I.73 ff. Dr Kirk does not directly mention problems of this kind in *Conscience and its Problems*.

[52] e.g. H. C. White, *The Metaphysical Poets* (1936), p. 59; L. L. Martz, *The Poetry of Meditation*, pp. 160 ff; C. Smyth, *Cambridge Review* (February 1947), p. 271.

be a more important question in the universe? And if this is, in the end, inscrutable, how can we live confidently and know God as children know their Father? A state of doubt as to our relationship with God cannot be healthy. Its unconscious misery may be worse for the soul than the most morbid introspection of the most individualistic evangelical. It may lead to frantic investment in any human nostrum or superstition.

The great Puritans were eminently sane in resolving this case of conscience. They did not appeal to subjective feelings or voices that may deceive. They began with God Himself and His election. Both Greenham and Gouge use the illustration of a man swimming. To quote Greenham: 'Againe, as a man swimming in the deepe waters is never in danger of drowning so long as his head continueth above the water: So though you swim in deep seas of dangerous temptations, yet are you sure and secure because Christ Jesus your head is still above all your troubles; and therefore able to draw you (his members) to the shoare of Salvation without all peril of perishing.'[53] It is because of our union with Christ that our salvation is sure. Walter Marshal, who expounds so intensively this mystical union, is certain that 'some assurance of our salvation' is the prerequisite of holiness; but it is not the kind of assurance which answers the question 'whether I am already in a state of grace and salvation' but rather 'whether God be graciously pleased now to bestow Christ and his salvation upon me, tho' I have been hitherto a very wicked Creature'. It is never an assurance of salvation irrespective of manner of life. It is the faith of which Christ speaks in the Gospels, the faith which so often seems to have been the channel of His healing power. The very fight of faith against doubt proves 'that there is and must be something of assurance of salvation in saving faith'.[54] Richard Baxter explains just what certainty and comfort such an act of faith in the love of God in Christ for sinners can afford: 'All the terrifying temptations which are grounded on misrepresentations of God, as if he were a cruel destroyer to be fled from, are dispelled by the due consideration of his goodness and the deep settled apprehension of his gracious, merciful, lovely nature.' The

---

[53] *A Garden of Spirituall Flowers;* cf. W. Gouge, *Workes*, II.56; Bolton, *Directions*, p. 23. John Donne says: 'It is enough that in this sea, God holds no man up by the chin so, but he that sin in confidence of that sustention shall sink' (*Fifty Sermons*, XXII.189 c). The Puritans would not have disagreed.

[54] *Gospel Mystery*, pp. 168 ff.

great general certainties which the Bible proclaims are the basis of individual assurance:

'Are you willing to have Christ to pardon, sanctify, guide and save you, or not? If you are, then you are a true believer and did not know it. If you are not, if you will but wait on God's word in hearing, reading, and consider frequently and seriously of the necessity and excellency of Christ and glory and the evil of sin and the vanity of the world, and will but beg earnestly of God to make you willing, you shall find that God hath not appointed you this means in vain, and that this way will be more profitable to you than all your complainings. See therefore when you are at your lowest that you forsake not the comforts of general grace.'

There is a logic, a syllogism, even here: 'God hath made a grant to every sinful man of pardon and salvation through Christ's sacrifice, if they will but repent and believe in Christ; But I am a sinful man, therefore God hath made this grant of pardon and salvation to me.'[55] We may compare the implicit syllogism of Hopeful's prayer in *Pilgrim's Progress:* 'Lord I have heard that thou art a merciful God, and hast ordained that thy Son Jesus Christ should be the Saviour of the World; and moreover that thou art willing to bestow him upon such a poor sinner as I am. And I am a sinner indeed. Lord, take therefore this opportunity and magnify thy grace in the salvation of my soul, through thy Son Jesus Christ, Amen.'[56] It is interesting to remember that John Wesley, who claimed that his doctrine of assurance was the same as that of the Puritans, also, in his sermon on the witness of the Spirit, sums up the matter in a syllogism:

He that now loves God, that delights and rejoices in Him with an humble joy, an holy delight, and an obedient love, is a child of God:
But I thus love, delight, and rejoice in God;
Therefore, I am a child of God.[57]

There are also outward signs of regeneration. The authors of *A Garden of Spirituall Flowers* list eight such 'Infallible Tokens'.

(1) A love to the children of God.
(2) A delight in His word.

[55] *Works*, IX.264-5.   [56] J. Bunyan, *Works*, III.155.
[57] *Standard Sermons* (1935 edn), I.210.

(3) Fervent prayer.
(4) Zeal of God's glory.
(5) Denial of ourselves.
(6) Patient bearing of the Cross.
(7) Faithfulness in our callings.
(8) Just and conscionable dealings.[58]

This teaching is not far removed from that of Richard Hooker: 'God hath left us infallible evidence whereby we may at any time give true and righteous sentence upon ourselves. We cannot examine the hearts of others, we may our own. "That we have passed from death to life, we know it," saith St John, "because we love our brethren." I trust beloved we know that we are not reprobates, because our spirit doth bear us record that the faith of our Lord Jesus Christ is in us.'[59]

The Puritan casuist knows, however, that there are wrong scruples, that sometimes we can cherish our doubts and forget that they may arise because repentance has been incomplete, and the evil, poisonous root of sin has never been torn from the soul.[60] Sometimes guilt of conscience is the result of sin through carelessness, the over-confident taking of too much liberty. Easy it is to leave the safe shore of rectitude and be out of our depth in sin before we are aware of it. Yet equally we may be, in the Authorized Version's use of the word 'superstitious', over-precise and punctilious, tortured in conscience over meat and clothes and secondary things, reaching out for a righteousness which we cannot attain, which is in fact the righteousness of the scribes and Pharisees, when it is God whom we are called to serve, 'with a single heart and eye'.[61] Evangelical assurance would seem to be the proper answer to scruples of this kind.

Baxter also knows how the Devil 'overdoes', and if he cannot pervert the saints by worldliness, seeks to make them more Christian than Christ.[62] Similarly, Walter Marshal says: 'That precept of *Solomon, Be not righteous overmuch,* is very useful and necessary if rightly understood. . . . Overdoing commonly proveth undoing.' If only Peter had accepted the Lord's merciful

---

[58] This is identical with Arthur Dent's 'Eight Infallible Notes and Tokens of a Regenerate Mind', in *A Plain Man's Pathway to Heaven* (London, 1601).
[59] Sermon I on St Jude, *Works* (1723 edn), p. 508.
[60] See R. Greenham, *Workes*, pp. 129 ff.
[61] The phrase is Charles Wesley's (*MHB*, No. 572).
[62] *Works*, IX.192.

dismissal of his weak disciples in St John's account of the passion, and not followed to the Judgement Hall, he would have been saved from denying Christ.[63]

Yet if we have examined ourselves honestly, and still groan and fear without consolation, we can at least believe that pain, however sharp it be, means life. Greenham would not have found Charles Wesley's prayer strange:

> *The sharpness of Thy two-edged sword*
> *Enable me to endure;*
> *Till bold to say: My hallowing Lord*
> *Hath wrought a perfect cure.*[64]

There is perhaps, for the Puritans, a dark night of the conscience. But nothing can overcome the surety that Christ died for such sins as ours. The malignant spirit who whispers that we are damned may be refuted by the promises. If that fails, says Greenham, send him to Christ who is our advocate.[65] We have not to defend ourselves. There is one who ever lives to plead the cause of the believing sinner. So the Puritans would give to the over-scrupulous the counsel which Staupitz gave to Luther, and which Luther so often repeated.

Some, like Bunyan, agonized long because they feared that they had committed the unforgivable sin against the Holy Spirit. Gouge has a treatise on the subject in which he explains the element of deliberate malice in this sin,[66] which he defines as 'despitefull rejecting of the Gospell after that the spirit hath supernaturally persuaded a man's heart of the truth and benefit thereof'. There can be no forgiveness for this—certainly not in the world to come, because it wilfully spurns the only means of pardon, which is Christ. The elect cannot fall into it, says Gouge —and here we tremble at what may be an intolerable antinomian-ism. But this is not quite as bad as it sounds, since the elect are those who have trusted in God and cling to His mercy. So Bunyan can say that they that *would* be saved by Christ cannot be counted as those who have sinned against the Spirit. No one who comes can be cast out, only he who deliberately counts Christ's works those of the Devil. If I see my lost condition, if I,

---

[63] *Gospel Mystery*, p. 265. [64] *MHB*, No. 556.
[65] *Workes*, p. 144. [66] *Workes*, I.271 ff.

however feebly, love Christ, then I am safe, for I love Him because He first loved me.[67]

Yet there is a note of caution in Richard Baxter. He fears 'the vain presumption of the natural mind', and knows how slowly the regenerate heart emerges from the darkness of self-deception to the light of Divine truth. He declares warningly: 'You much mistake (and those who tell you so), if you think that the spirit of adoption lieth only in a persuasion that you are God's child, or that you may not have the spirit of adoption without such a persuasion of God's adopting you. For God may adopt you and give you that spirit which he gives only to his children and possess you with true filial affections toward him, before ever you know yourself to be adopted; much more though you may have frequent doubts of your adoption'.[68] Nevertheless, Baxter insists that lack of complete assurance does not imply a lack of Christian consolation: 'Trouble of mind may be overcome; conscience may be quieted; true peace obtained; yea a man may have that joy in the Holy Ghost wherein the kingdom of God is said to consist, without certainty of salvation.'[69] This is his revised and considered judgement.

---

[67] *The Jerusalem Sinner Saved, Works*, I.102 ff.   [68] *Works*, IX.55.   [69] ibid., p. 101.

The next day they took him, and had him into the armoury, where they showed him all manner of furniture which their Lord had provided for pilgrims, as sword, shield, helmet, breastplate, all-prayer, and shoes that would not wear out.

JOHN BUNYAN

Now let me gain perfection's height,
Now let me into nothing fall,
Be less than nothing in Thy sight,
And feel that Christ is all in all.

CHARLES WESLEY

CHAPTER EIGHT

PERSEVERANCE AND PERFECTION

WE have earlier noticed something of the inevitable tension in the Christian life between God's free grace and man's costly effort, the peace which is Christ's legacy to His own and the conflicts with which the soul is surrounded. The Puritans would have agreed with Luther that 'no one who has not experienced it can believe how great a cross it is to have a bad conscience, which is death itself and hell'.[1] The aim of their casuistry was to bring 'the labouring conscience peace' by the application of the Gospel of grace and holiness. They believed that the assurance of our standing with God is the great incentive to the spiritual combat. They did not conceive of the Christian life as a joyless journey through 'a forbidding and frost-bound wilderness rolling its snow-clad leagues toward the grave'.[2] Man's natural instincts were not to be inhibited, but restored to the purposes for which the Creator had endowed them. The mixed dancing of men and women as practised in that age too often seemed to be an incitement to lasciviousness,[3] but Bunyan's Christian danced for the joy of his redemption. There are many passages in our authors which reveal their delight in music, admittedly the least sensuous of the arts.[4] Just as the Temple of old was filled with music and musicians, so must the Christian life be a psalm of praise. 'An uncomfortable Gospel cannot proceed from God the Father, who is the Father of Mercies, and God of all comfort. Nor from Christ who is the consolation of Israel, nor from the Spirit who is the Comforter. . . . No sorrow is approved of by God except godly sorrow, which can

---

[1] *Letters of Spiritual Counsel* (ed. Tappert), p. 68.

[2] R. H. Tawney, *Religion and the Rise of Capitalism* (Pelican edn), p. 178.

[3] cf. W. Perkins, *Cases of Conscience, Workes*, II.141.

[4] e.g. the songs of Bunyan's pilgrims, and Baxter's frequent references to singing and praise in the *Saint's Everlasting Rest*. W. Ames, *Conscience*, Book IV.43 f. See Percy A. Scholes, *The Puritans and Music* (Oxford, 1934).

never be in us, without some comfort of the love of God towards us.'[5]

TEMPTATION AND CONFLICT

Nevertheless there is a warfare to the Christian upon earth. In all ages, Christian spirituality has used metaphors from the battle-field. Puritan writers allegorized the battles of the Old Testament, and there were many treatises which placed the individual's conflict in the setting of the universal cosmic war between Christ and the Devil.[6] Richard Baxter, for instance, writes of the two great armies which confront each other throughout history.[7] The same idea underlies Ignatius Loyola's *Meditation on Two Standards*.[8] But Jesuit and Puritan alike realized that the warfare is psychological. The analogy of combat depicts clearly the state of alertness in which Christians should live, and the counsellors go on to expose the stratagems of the enemy.

Temptations may be due to the direct machinations of Satan the accuser. The Puritans expound these in Augustinian terms.[9] They have much to say about the tempter's use of the imagination: 'This imagination of ours is become the seat of vanity, and thereupon a vexation to us, because it apprehends a greater happiness in outward good things than there is, and a greater misery in outward evil things than indeed there is.'[10] Evil desire, seizing the imagination, infects the will, and it is that alone which capitulates or resists. Temptation can use almost any occasion or propensity of life: bodily weakness, choleric temperament, social conventions, the spur of fame, even the desire of virtue.[11] Satan often appears as an angel of light. If his subtlety is understood and the weakness of our nature known, and if the powers of our being, imagination, and desire turn to the obedience of God, then we shall have armour against him. But the surest way to triumph is to refer Satan to Christ, who lives to succour us and is the great Captain in the fight. We ought to take comfort from the

---

[5] W. Marshal, *Gospel Mystery*, p. 166.
[6] See W. Haller, *Rise of Puritanism*, pp. 151-3, for an account. We disagree with his statement that the military eclipsed the mystical in Puritan writings.
[7] *Works*, II.260.
[8] *Spiritual Exercises*, pp. 100 ff.
[9] cf. P. Pourrat, *Christian Spirituality*, pp. 199 ff.
[10] R. Sibbes, *Works*, I.179.
[11] cf. Baxter, ibid., pp. 263 ff.

very fact of having spiritual struggles, for they are the signs that we have not yielded to sin. Richard Greenham uses a country illustration to explain Satan's impotence against believers: 'For as the humming Bee having lost her sting in another doth still, not withstanding, make a fearefull and grievous noyse, by her often buzzing about us, but is nothing able to hurt us; so sinne and death having lost their stings in Christ Jesus, doe not cease at all even in the height of the parching heate of our consciences, to make a murmuring; and with furious storms of temptation to terrifie us and our consciences, albeit they never sting us.'[12]

There are also temptations which come from God himself. These are not to provoke us to evil, 'but to trie in what measure we have profited by his mercies'.[13] Benefits and afflictions alike can either lure us to Satan or crown the work of grace in our hearts. We must indeed always walk in fear and trembling. 'If the force of Temptations could bring him which had no sinne of his owne and was the only beloved of God, and which had received the spirit of fortitude above measure to such hard and terrible conflict, we ought not to meruaile if the children of God which have sinne dwelling in their mortall bodies, which are not beloved for themselves but for his sake alone and which have received but of a droppe of the Spirit (whereof he had the whole Sea), be sometimes plunged overhead and eares.'[14]

There are no trials more severe than those of human suffering, but the Puritans had great belief in the purifying power of afflictions. Paul Baynes is fond of saying that God can turn 'vipers into triacles'.[15] The problem of pain did not preoccupy the Puritans as it does men today. 'Soundly believe the promises of Christ', says Baxter, 'and then you will never much stick at suffering.'[16] The Puritans believed with Scripture that for the child of God suffering was contingent upon the divine ordinance. It was He who sent sickness and sorrow, not chance or fortune.[17] They thus tried to receive the bitter cup as from the hands of a merciful Father, and they believed that the Cross of Christ had transformed everything, so that in Him our lighter crosses and punishments were only means of discipline.[18] This view is only

---

[12] *Workes* (3rd edn, 1601), p. 144.   [13] ibid., p. 437.

[14] P. Baynes, *Christian Letters*, unpaginated.   [15] ibid.

[16] *Works*, XXX.376.   [17] cf. *A Garden of Spirituall Flowers.*

[18] cf. W. Perkins, *Christ Crucified, Workes*, I.753.

harsh if it is thrust sanctimoniously upon other people, or elevated into a philosophy of religion. Accepted 'existentially', it is a strength to Christians who bear the cross after Christ. Milton's sonnet 'On His Blindness' should be mentioned here, not because it is 'typical'—as we have seen, there is danger of misjudging both the Puritans and Milton if we ever so regard him—but because of the austere nobility of its devotion, a corrective to the sentimentality which sometimes surrounds even the Crucified. It is not to the historic Cross that Milton turns for comfort—maybe he would not so presume—but to the transcendent majesty of God, whose purposes are not defeated because His human servants cannot serve Him as they had hoped.

> *God doth not need*
> *Either man's work, or His own gifts; who best*
> *Bear His mild yoke, they serve Him best: His state*
> *Is kingly; thousands at His bidding speed,*
> *And post o'er land and ocean without rest;*
> *They also serve who only stand and wait.*

Toward the end of his life, Richard Baxter came increasingly to believe that suffering is the Church's *métier*, 'even when there are none but formal, nominal Christians to be the cross-makers, and though ordinarily God would have vicissitudes of summer and winter, day and night, that the Church may grow extensively in the summer of prosperity and intensively in the winter of adversity, yet usually their night is longer than their day, and that day itself hath its storms and tempests'.[19]

One way of pursuing the spiritual conflict was by the discipline of fasting. A book which is typical of the Puritan attitude is *The Holy Exercise of a True Fast*, published in 1610, and considered to be the work of Thomas Cartwright, sometime Lady Margarets Professor of Divinity at Cambridge, and first leader of the Puritans.[20] The author is anxious that discipline shall not disappear with Rome, any more than the Sabbath with the Jews. The Romans indeed abuse fasting, and feast on all manner of delicacies during their apparent abstinence. True fasting should consist both of 'outward ceremony' and inward humiliation, the

[19] Quoted from *Reliquinae Baxterianae* by Alan Simpson, *Puritanism in Old and New England*, p. 98.
[20] A. Peel and L. H. Carson, *Cartwrightiana* (1951), pp. 118-55.

former to give the soul 'a wing for heaven'. Fasting means mortification, not as a pharisaical work, but as a crucifixion of the flesh to be joined with prayer. There should be no mechanical rule in the matter, but fasting should be according to need, and especially at times of God's wrath. It must not interfere with duties, nor include the dishonouring of the body by scourging and mutilation.

WHITHER ASSURANCE LEADS

The question arises: 'What did the Puritans teach about the goal of the Christian life and its attainment?' Many of them, like the poet Richard Crashaw's father, William, regarded it as Romanist heresy that perfection should be deemed attainable in this life.[21] The sober counsellors and pastors may have been too conscious of the little progress the generality of the people made to have shared the full 'optimism of grace'. Moreover, the Puritans distrusted the perfectionist 'antinomian' groups. These are represented by William Dell, one of Cromwell's chaplains, whom Wesley included in the *Christian Library*, and who said in a sermon preached before the Commons in 1646 that man's reformation 'once begun is never intermitted till all be perfected. For as long as God's nature dwelles in ours, it will ever be reforming our nature to itself till it be altogether like it.'[22] Walter Marshal attacks the doctrine of perfection, because, he says, it 'hardens people to allow themselves in sin, and call evil good'.[23] It discourages those who seek holiness by faith, for it makes them think that they labour in vain when sin rears its head against them. It makes men crave a holiness which is not of faith, to demand a short cut to Heaven, where none is saved by bodily death. Christ's work is not limited because the full realization of perfect love must wait for the hereafter. He never intended that His merits should enable us in this life to go beyond faith.

The Calvinist alternative to perfectionism was the doctrine of 'the Final Perseverance of the Saints'. Apostasy was deemed impossible for those in a state of grace. This was challenged and defended in a battle of weighty tomes between John Goodwin

---

[21] cf. W. Crashaw, *The Jesuits' Gospell* (1621).
[22] Quoted by Gertrude Huehns, *Antinomianism in English History* (1951), p. 38; cf. W. Haller, *Liberty and Reformation*, pp. 200 ff.
[23] *Gospel Mystery*, p. 243.

and John Owen. In *Redemption Redeemed,* John Goodwin advanced the Arminian belief in universal redemption, and, as a corollary, was compelled to assert that it is possible to fall from grace. God wills all men to be saved, Christ died for all, but men are free to accept or reject his saving work. The doctrine that justification is immutable, and that therefore believers continue in grace to the end of their lives seems to Goodwin to be 'a promising to all men, and that with height of assurance, under what looseness of vile practises soever, exemption and freedom from punishment'.[24] We may sympathize with Owen's retort that this is a caricature of the doctrine, and with his grounding of 'final perseverance' on the compassion of Christ for His own, and on the promise of Scripture that nothing can separate us from the love of God in Christ.

'Or doth the doctrine which teaches believers (saints, who have tasted of the love and pardoning mercy of God, and are taught to value it infinitely above all the world) that such is the love and goodwill of God toward them in the Covenant of mercy in the blood of Christ, that having appointed good works for them to walk in, for which of themselves they are insufficient, he will graciously continue to them such supplies of his Spirit and grace as that they shall never depart from following after him in ways of gospel obedience—doth this, I say, encourage any of them to continue in sin that grace may abound?'[25]

It is significant that both Arminian and Calvinist regard each other's doctrines as tending to antinomianism. Owen thrusts shrewdly when he argues that evangelical truth is not invalidated because carnal hearts turn it into wantonness.[26] The real point at issue is which of the rival doctrines is evangelically true? Both seek to resolve the antinomy of freedom and omnipotence; the one safeguards the initiative of God, the other the need for human response and for a real change of heart in believers; the one is in dire peril of limiting the mercy of God, the other may go to seed in the worst excesses of subjective revivalism.

Yet the Puritans were too faithful to Scripture to ignore its teaching of perfection. And so Richard Greenham, while sure that there is no absolute unspottedness in this life, goes on to add:

[24] Quoted by J. Owen, *Works,* XI.99.   [25] ibid., p. 101.   [26] ibid., p. 102.

'Albeit to that perfection which the Scripture taketh for sound-
nesse, trueth, and sinceritie of heart, which is void of carelesse
remisness wee may come.'[27]

It is, as we should expect, John Preston who gives us most fully
what we are seeking. The passionate desire for Christ which we
have seen in his soliloquy and treatises of Divine Love is not of the
kind that can rest content with a partial benefit, even in this life.
In his sermons, published under the title of *The New Covenant*,
he expounds the word of God to Abraham which the Geneva
Bible renders: 'I am God All-Sufficient; Walke before me and be
thou perfect.'[28] He says 'every man is more or less perfect as he
is more or lesse perswaded of God's All-Sufficiencie', and after a
lengthy exposition of the similitude between a Christian's life
and a journey on foot, which occupies almost a whole sermon,
he comes to his next main point: 'Whosoever hath interest in
God's All-sufficiencie, must be a perfect man.'[29] Perfection is
integrity of heart, says Preston, and can exist along with those
infirmities which are an inevitable part of our humanity. Otherwise the second Adam would be less powerful to instil grace
than the first to communicate sin, and the work of God in the
new creation would come short of that in the beginning, when the
Lord looked on everything that he had made, and behold it was
very good. We dare not limit the redemption wrought by Christ.
Preston recognizes that there are degrees of perfection: 'There is a
perfection of the bud and a perfection of the flower.' This, a
favourite metaphor of expositors of Wesley, is paralleled in
Preston's words:

'So this is true of the workes of Redemption, of the workes of God in a
man's heart, of destroying the workes of Sathan, and setting up a new
building, which is the work of Jesus Christ, and the end, for which he
came; I say this is true of it, it is perfect, it wants onely growth: As, you
may say, it is a perfect seed, when it is ripe it will be a perfect flower;
or it is a perfect plant, when it growes up, it will be a perfect tree, it is
perfect in all respects. Such a perfection is in the workes of Redemption,
and, if the heart of man be not entire, if the work of grace be not
throughout, if there bee a defect in the principle, & constitution of it,

---

[27] *Workes*, p. 134.

[28] Genesis 17[1]. It is interesting that Bede Frost quotes these very words which
'express clearly in what our perfection *in via* is to consist' (*Art of Mental Prayer*, p. 27).

[29] op. cit., p. 214.

there should be a defect in the workes of Redemption, which indeed cannot be.'[30]

There is a further reason why perfection of heart must be wrought in all the saved. Apart from this the commands of the Gospel would be impossible, for unless we can keep them in a sincere, evangelical manner they are nonsense, and the covenant between God and us is not reciprocal; it would be no covenant at all if we could not answer His all-sufficiency with our obedience. This conception of the Christian law separates Preston from the modern dialectical theologians, and from Dr Reinhold Niebuhr, who regards it as heresy to imagine that the moral imperatives of the Gospel can be completely realized.[31]

The perfect heart is the single heart. If we want to test our own hearts, we can do so by the commands to perfection in the Gospel.[32] 'If thou wilt be perfect,' said Jesus to the young man, in words that have echoed down the centuries, 'go sell all that thou hast.' This says Preston, means that we must be willing to suffer any calamity in the world, to part with any blessing for Christ. If we love bodily freedom, wife and children, reputation, trade, more than Him we have a 'rotten heart'. The second test is in the words: 'Be ye therefore perfect, as your heavenly Father is perfect.' 'Beloved, the meaning of this is not that you should reach his perfection; for who can ever doe it? But the meaning of it is this, there must be as great a length, as great a breadth, and latitude in your perfection as in his, your perfection must answer his.'[33] There must be no maimed obedience to God's commandments, we must love our *enemies*, even as our heavenly Father makes His sun to shine on good and bad alike; we must not swear the smallest oaths; we must not cherish sinful lusts, and must forgive perfectly. We must honour the least of God's commandments.

The holy man may relapse into sin, but there is all the difference in the world between the backsliding of him whose heart is unsound, and the failures of him whose heart is perfect with God. The latter is strengthened in virtue even by his sin; he profits from his mistakes. The godly man makes no excuses for his sin, and the

---

[30] op. cit., p. 216.
[31] See e.g. *The Nature and Destiny of Man*, II.175 ff.
[32] J. Preston, op. cit., p. 236.
[33] ibid., p. 239.

spirit of holiness rises up within him like a strong current bearing
him relentlessly from the opposing streams. And it is only when he
is possessed by evil, and, momentarily, no longer himself, that he
errs. According to Preston, Romans 7 could be the experience
of a perfect man.

'A sheepe may fall into the myre as soone as a swine, for the commission of sin, and so likewise for the omission of duties; an Appletree
may have a fit of barrenes and unfruitfulnes, as well as a Crabtree, or
any other, but the difference is great in the maner of them as we
shewed: But still the maine difference is to be remembered, that hee
that hath a perfect heart, is still cleansing and purifying himselfe; the
other doe not that, but so fall backe to sinne, that they wallow in it,
as a swine doth in the myre.'[34]

All might be summed up in the words of the Apostle: 'Not as
though I had already attained, either were already perfect:
But I follow after, if that I may apprehend that for which also I
am apprehended of Christ Jesus. . . . I press toward the mark for
the prize of the high calling of God in Christ Jesus. Let us, therefore, as many as be perfect, be thus minded.'[35] The paradox of
Christian perfection is that the man who thus with a single eye
and pure heart looks to the goal of perfect love has arrived even
while he travels on.

Despite the differences of theological emphasis within Puritanism, there is little outward difference of piety. Whether salvation
is conceived of as all of God's irresistible electing grace, or as a
union of God's free offer and man's free acceptance, life is a
serious business. It is not a game for us to play. Whether faith
or love is considered the paramount spiritual gift, there is, in union
with Christ, a security which the rude shocks of mortal life cannot
disturb. It is not a game that is being played on us! Therefore we
can be glad. Yet the measure is more often grave than light.
The Puritans do not condemn recreation, not even 'sporting,
pleasant and recreative talk'.[36] But moderation, the service of
God, and a just regard for our neighbour, must govern all. Nothing in life must be enterprised or taken in hand lightly, inadvisedly

---

[34] op. cit., p. 258.   [35] Philippians 3[12-15].   [36] Baxter, *Works*, III.613 ff.

L

or wantonly; there can be no real relaxation in the good fight. It is with this question that Baxter confronts those who would regard gaming and stage plays as not unlawful—set yourselves as dying men in the presence of God and contemplate frivolities if you can!

Now it belongs not to my care
  Whether I die or live;
To love and serve Thee is my share,
  And this Thy grace must give.

If life be long, I will be glad
  That I may long obey;
If short, yet why should I be sad
  To soar to endless day?

Christ leads me through no darker rooms
  Than he went through before;
He that into God's kingdom comes
  Must enter by this door.

Come, Lord, when grace has made me meet
  Thy blessèd face to see;
For if Thy work on earth be sweet
  What will Thy glory be?

Then shall I end my sad complaints,
  And weary, sinful days,
And join with the triumphant saints
  That sing Jehovah's praise.

My knowledge of that life is small,
  The eye of faith is dim;
But it's enough that Christ knows all,
  And I shall be with Him.

RICHARD BAXTER

CHAPTER NINE

HOLY DYING

'THINK often', counsels Bayly, 'of the shortness of thy life.'[1] In an age of 'battle, and murder, and sudden death', to say nothing of pestilence, and perilous child-birth, there were constant reminders of mortality. Death is no respecter of religious profession, and for both Catholics and Protestants life was a rehearsal of dying. All spiritual writers devote much space to instructing their readers how to die well.

Indeed, we may describe this as the purpose of all the Puritan guides to a holy life. John Preston's *Grace to the Humble*, printed 'by Tho. Cotes for Michael Sparke Jnr.' for sale 'at the signe of the blue Bible, in Green Arbor', 1639, bears as its frontispiece a picture of the volume and an hour-glass with an angel on one side and a skeleton on the other, and, beneath, the words:

> *The Glasse doth Runne and Time doth Go*
> *Study me in thy Prime*
> *Bury Death and Weary Time.*

The medieval fear of the last things still possessed men's minds. No greater contrast to the philosophic calm of Socrates about to drink the hemlock, or of Francis Bacon's declaration, 'It is as natural to die as to be born', can be found than the attitude of seventeenth-century Christian orthodoxy. So much was this the case that Robert Bolton suggests meditations to master the immoderate fear of death, quoting Samuel Ward: 'The pangs of death are often lesse than of the toothache.'[2]

PREPARATION FOR DEATH

William Perkins's *Salve for a Sicke Man or a Treatise containing the Nature, Differences, and Kindes of death, as also the right manner of dying well* is particularly designed for 'Marriners when they goe to

---

[1] *The Practice of Piety*, p. 133.　　[2] R. Bolton, *Foure Last Things*, p. 62.

sea: Souldiers when they goe to battell: Women when they travell of child'—three dangerous occupations indeed![3]

Master Perkins bases his expositions on Ecclesiastes 7[1]: 'The day of death is better than the day that one is borne.' He is not aware of the cynicism of the canonical author, but sees him as a type and forerunner of Christian saint. Since 'death is deprivation of life and a punishment ordained of God and imposed on man for his sin', how is it conceivable that the day of dying be the happiest of all? Perkins explains that there are two kinds of death—our passage from this life, which is the separation of body and soul, and the second a spiritual death in which the whole man—if his sins have brought in this dreadful stipend—is separated to all eternity from the gracious fellowship of God. This spiritual death has three degrees: when a man still lives on earth, but, 'is dead in trespasses and sins'; when at the end of his life, the sinful soul descends into the place of torment; and finally, when at the last judgement, soul and body meet again to be consigned to everlasting damnation.[4]

Perkins's text concerns bodily death. And this, through Christ, becomes for the righteous the wicket-gate to heaven. No screaming agonies at the last can deny this. God who created the world out of nothing, and who brings life out of death, often sends his servants to heaven from the very gates of hell. 'The love of God is like a sea into which a man is cast, he neither feeles bottom nor sees banke.' We are not to judge of a man by the mode of his death, but by his life. A sudden death is not so much to be feared as an evil life.

Like spiritual death, eternal life has its three degrees. It can begin here and now, when 'Christ liveth in me'; the soul experiences it in greater fullness from the moment of bodily death; its completion is at the Last Judgement. We are not to think that the dissolution of the soul and body is for the Christian a severance from Christ. By his death and burial Christ has made our graves 'of stinking and loathesome cabins to become princely pallaces and beds of most sweet and happy rest, far more excellent than beds of downe'. 'The whole person of man both in bodie and soule is joyned and united to whole Christ', so that 'rotting in the

---

[3] *Workes*, I.587 ff, from which all citations unless otherwise noted.

[4] cf. Lewis Bayly's lurid dialogue of the reunion of damned body and soul, *Practice of Piety*, p. 46. This is thoroughly medieval.

grave, drowned in the sea, burned to ashes' it 'abides still united
to him, and is as truely a member of Christ then as before.'
Burial in the grave may be a winter season for the body, but it will
bud again, since it is joined to the Eternal Root. The wicked
indeed rise again at the last day, but this is by Christ's power to
judgement. For the righteous, death is hallowed into sleep.
'Beeing once certainely assured in conscience of our beeing in
Christ, let death come when it will and let it cruelly part asunder
both bodie and soule, yet shal they both remain in the Covenant
and by means thereof be reunited and taken up to life eternall.'[5]

The ever-practical Perkins now goes on to the preparations
for death. 'As death leaveth a man so shall the last judgement
find him.' Holy living is thus the surest preparation. Perkins
distrusts late repentance as seldom true (i.e. sincere), being
constrained more by fears of hell than love of God. He argues,
soundly enough, that the case of the dying thief is extraordinary.
It is less satisfying when he also maintains that the thief's repentance was in order to show forth Christ's power and virtue, as
though the whole were contrived, stage-managed in fact, by a
celestial producer.

However, this is a mere aside, and Perkins continues with the
need both of a right use of time, and of entering even now the first
degree of life eternal. We should regard the affliction and
hardships of our calling as a preparation for death, learning with
St Paul to 'die daily'. Perkins tells of the reformer Thomas
Bilncy, who would put his finger into a candle flame that he might
prepare himself for the fires of martyrdom.[6] This reveals a rather
different attitude to suffering from that of the Catholic saint who
regards pain as something to be offered to God with the Passion
of Christ. For the Puritan, it was more a disciplinary hardness of
the pilgrim way; its surmounting brought heaven nearer.

The Puritan idiom becomes most apparent when the writers

[5] cf. Bolton, *Foure Last Things*, p. 6: 'The godly man ... shall most certainly upon
his dying bed meete with a glorious troupe of blessed Angels; ready and rejoycing to
guard and conduct his departing Soule into his Master's joy. His body shall be
preserved in the grave by the all powerful providence, as in a cabinet of rest and
sweetest sleepe, perfumed by the buriall of our blessed Saviour, untill the glorious
appearing of the Great God . . . and then, after their joyfullest reunion, they shall
both be filled and shine thorow all eternity, with such glory and blisse, which in
sweetnesse and excellency doth infinitely exceed the possibility of all humane or
Angelicall conceipt.'

[6] For an account of Bilney and his martyrdom see E. G. Rupp, *The English Protestant
Tradition*, esp. pp. 22-31.

turn to the onrush of death itself. Perkins will have no truck with sacramental confession. Communion of the sick is likely to degenerate into making private what is the act of the people of God; in any case the devout receiving of the Supper among God's people extends to the whole of life afterwards.

Perkins anticipates modern theologians in his attitude to the co-operation of divinity and medicine.[7] We may say that he is all for the orthodox in both and condemns superstitious quackery. But he is anxious that prayer should not be regarded as a last resort when the physicians have failed. Indeed it should be the very opposite! 'Where the Divine ends there the physitian must begin.' Let the minister be summoned first in sickness, for often the malady will be accentuated by a disordered soul, and there can be no true health until the patient is right with God. The physician himself should be able to act as a member of Christ.

It is not, however, sufficient merely to have the counsel of the minister. Church members must come to the sick-bed, and be prepared to be more than casual, worldly comforters. The dying man should meditate more on heaven than hell, and be sustained with the great promises of New Testament and Old: 'Blessed are the dead which die in the Lord'[8] and 'When thou passest through the waters I will be with thee.'[9] Neither must temporal dispositions be forgotten—to die intestate, or to leave earthly responsibilities untended is a sin. And Perkins cannot resist providing also a catalogue of the dreadful dying agonies of the apostate, perhaps forgetting the wisdom of his earlier assurance that the manner of death is no authentic augury of the soul's condition.

In their disapproval of Communion to the sick and dying, Perkins and the Puritans generally are departing from Calvin's wishes.[10] The insistence that Church members should surround sick-beds emphasized the priestly nature of the whole society, in contrast with the Catholic assertion of the prerogatives of a certain caste within it to give absolution. We may perhaps claim that this

[7] e.g. H. H. Farmer, *The World and God*, p. 263; cf. Greenham, *Workes*, p. 137: 'For my part, I would never have the phisition's counsell severed nor the minister's labour neglected; because the soule and the bodie dwelling together, it is convenient, that as the soule should be cured by the worde by prayer, by fasting, by threatening or by comforting; so the bodie also should be brought into some temperature by phisicke, by purging, by diet, by restoring, by musicke, and by such like meanes.'

[8] Revelation 13[14].

[9] Isaiah 43[1-2].

[10] See W. D. Maxwell, *John Knox's Genevan Service Book* (1556), p. 56.

convention influenced the change in the attitude to death which the subsequent century and a half witnessed. 'Death to the eighteenth-century dissenter was not only the last enemy but the first friend. It was a glorious adventure, an experience to be envied by others and not feared by the saints. The Puritan fear of death had softened by this time to a sentimental semi-Calvinistic concept.'[11] The act and moment of dying became transfigured as friends at the bedside bent earnestly to catch the saint's last groans. It was indeed good doctrine that the believer should die in the congregation, even as he was baptized into it; yet it is obvious that the custom would add excitement to the mortal passage and encourage the death-bed scenes which became at their worst a revolting feature of later evangelicalism.[12]

In summarizing Perkins's short work—it is in fact an extended sermon—we have given but one example of a literature which is inexhaustible. Many Puritan guides give pattern prayers for the sick and dying. Some of these will concern us when we come to consider below the doctrine of the future state. But there is nothing distinctive to Puritan piety about this elaborate prepara-tion for death. At the end of the seventeenth century, we find a non-Juror, Nathaniel Spinckes, in *The Sick Man Visited*, describing in detail six visits to a dying man, all devoted to preparation for death, and concluding with suitable meditations and prayers. So intense did such meditations become, in health as well as in sickness, that Walter Marshal has to point out that 'looking on the Picture of Death or on a Death's-head, keeping a Coffin by them ready made, walking about among the graves, &c. . . . is not the manner of living to God, whereof the apostle speaketh when he saith, "I live, yet not I but Christ liveth in me; and the life that I now live in the flesh I live by the faith of the Son of God, who loved me and gave himself for me".'[13] The counsel of the com-posite manual, *A Garden of Spirituall Flowers*, however, is not calculated to induce a morbid but a comforting preparation.

---

[11] A. P. Davis, *Isaac Watts*, p. 68, cf. Isaac Watts, *Hymns and Spiritual Songs* (1731 edn), Part I.18, and the notorious hymn of Charles Wesley's, 'Ah lovely appearance of death'! which still appeared in the *Methodist Hymn-book* as late as 1875.

[12] They were deprecated by the nineteenth-century evangelical Charles Simeon (Charles Smyth, *Simeon and Church Order*, p. 312). R. A. Knox, *Enthusiasm*, p. 540, suggests that the passing of John Wesley did not provide one of the typically rapturous death-bed scenes of the Methodist Revival, but he ignores the singing of 'I'll praise my Maker'. In any case, Wesley was never an exhibitionist.

[13] *Gospel Mystery*, p. 251.

'Endeavour even to die praying; when thou art in the depth of miseries and at the gates of death, there is a depth of God's mercy which is ready to appeare and helpe thee: Misery must call upon Mercy.'

THE FUTURE STATE

As Perkins makes clear, the Puritans believed that the final destiny of the individual is determined at death, when the body is laid in the grave to await the general resurrection and last judgement, and the soul goes either to everlasting pleasures or pains.[14] There is nothing in the whole universe which corresponds to the Catholic purgatory. The state between bodily death and the general resurrection is intermediate in the sense that souls and bodies are sundered, and God's purpose is not finally complete. His judgement is not yet fully revealed and clearly seen, but sentence is pronounced, and the righteous need no further purification. The Puritans still remembered the abuse of purgatory, 'the gainfulest lie in all Popery',[15] but it is on theological grounds that the belief is unanimously condemned. The whole notion seemed to dishonour Christ as mediator, to assail the efficacy of His precious blood. Isaac Ambrose preached a sermon on 'Right Purgatory' from Hebrews 1³: 'When he (Christ) had himself purged our sins.' 'Hath Christ satisfied for us, and must we now make satisfaction for ourselves?' cries Henry Smith.[16] The same preacher's prayer for a sick man shows his belief about the matter. The invalid prays for health, because he knows that he has as yet done nothing for God on earth. 'But Lord, thou knowest what is best of all; and if thou convert me, I shall be converted in an hour; and as thou acceptest the will of David as well as the act of Solomon, so thou wilt accept my desire to serve thee as well as if I did live to glorify thee.'[17] John Preston insists more than once that 'all men are divided into two rankes, ... either they are good or bad, either they are polluted or cleane, either they are such as sacrifice or such as sacrifice not'. Therefore 'there is no Purgatorie or Limbus, either for the Fathers before Christ, or for children now'.[18]

This is noble doctrine. For believers in election it is inevitable —as Preston declares, men are saved or damned, and if saved there is no partial salvation, and if damned no partial damnation.

---

[14] See Thomas Goodwin, *Works*, Vol. VII.   [15] H. Smith, *Works*, I.266.
[16] ibid.   [17] ibid., II.467.   [18] *The New Covenant*, p. 507.

There are, however, several questions which need asking, though we must remember throughout that the medieval doctrine of purgatory in no sense mitigated the horrors of the medieval hell. It was 'to most minds simply old hell writ small',[19] and the humane theologian can at least feel that the Puritans rid the universe of one chamber of horrors. But they believed in the medieval hell, worm, fire and brimstone. How can such a hell be anything other than the defeat of the purpose revealed in Christ as the punishment of the lost runs parallel in eternity with the blessedness of the saved? How can God's will be thought to triumph in what Robert Bolton describes of the everlasting curses of the damned, 'even blaspheming of God himself blessed for ever?'[20]

Yet even while we deprecate such detail we must pause to reflect that it was a sign of the intensity of Puritan religious experience, and although its exalting into a cosmology is to be deplored, it may well be, as Henri Talon recognizes in the case of Bunyan, the interpretation of final destiny in terms of the spiritual conflict and torment of this life. Some of the Puritans believed in hell because they had been there, and if hell is a real state of the soul, it is understandable that, with the world view of the seventeenth century, it would be given a local habitation beyond the grave. The mistake is when the sense of alienation expressed in the poetic symbolism of the spiritual genius is translated too crudely into literal warning for the wayfaring man and the little children.[21]

John Bunyan, however, reconciles damnation with the divine justice and mercy in a remarkable passage of *The Jerusalem Sinner Saved*:

I have often thought of the day of judgement, and how God will deal with sinners at that day; and I believe it will be managed with that sweetness, with that equitableness, with that excellent righteousness as to every sin, and circumstance and aggravation thereof, that men that are damned shall, before judgement is over, receive such conviction of the righteous judgement of God upon them, and of their desert of

[19] G. G. Coulton, *Five Centuries of Religion*, I.73.
[20] *Foure Last Things*, p. 95.
[21] H. Talon, *John Bunyan*, p. 89. The work of Bunyan particularly in mind is *A Few sighs from Hell*, *Works*, III.666 ff. For nineteenth-century Catholic teaching on Hell see the children's books of Father Furniss, especially *The Sight of Hell*; 'The Fifth Dungeon, *The Red-Hot Oven*' (see C. Smyth, *Church and Parish*, p. 249, n.25).

hell-fire, that they shall in themselves conclude, that there is all the reason in the world that they should be shut out of heaven, and go to hell-fire: "These shall go away to everlasting punishment." [22]

Modern theologians, especially those of a philosophic turn, and not always of a Catholic persuasion, have argued in favour of belief in a state of purgation—that is of cleansing, if need be by pain—after death.[23] Is there in reality that clear moral division between personalities which Preston states, and which an in- dividualist interpretation of the parable of the sheep and the goats would maintain? Von Hügel argued that repentance and grace do not extirpate here the root of sin which indeed is not a growth extraneous to our being, but our very self, the complex of our habits and inclinations. God, in this life, changes us slowly and by long self-discipline, and why should the work of grace com- pletely alter its mode of operation because of bodily death? Moreover, what of those who live their mortal lives without knowledge of salvation? The Puritan would say that those elected are judged according to their light and Christ can be revealed to them in an instant at the hour of death; but again, if so, the spiritual laws of the next world seem totally different from those of this.[24]

This, according to the Puritan, reckons without justification by faith. The death of Jesus opens a new universe to believers, and with Him as Intercessor, and as Bridegroom of the soul, there can be no vague, intermediate acceptance with God. 'For by means of this your matching with Christ, you are become one with him and one in him; you dwell in him and he in you; he is your well- beloved and you are his. So that the marriage union betwixt Christ and you is more than a bare notion or apprehension of your mind, for it is a special spiritual and real union; it is a union betwixt the nature of Christ (God and Man) and you; it is a knitting and closing not only of your apprehension with a Saviour, but of your soul with a Saviour. Whence it must needs follow that you cannot be damned except Christ be damned with you, neither can Christ be saved, except ye be saved with him.'[25]

[22] *Works*, I.86.
[23] See F. von Hügel, *Mystical Element*, II.230 ff, for instances of changed feeling before 1908, and a brief history of the doctrine.
[24] See F. von Hügel, *Essays and Addresses*, II.202-3; cf. A. E. Taylor, *The Faith of a Moralist*, II.317 ff.
[25] *The Marrow of Moderne Divinity* (1902 edn), p. 134. Passages are incorporated from Thomas Hooker. The second edition is dated 1646.

The believer shares in Christ's death, and in His Resurrection and Ascension, and there can be no more descent into purgatory than Christ descended into hell after the Resurrection. We are reminded of the mystics' assertion that to be with Christ in hell would be heaven, and of one of Charles Wesley's allusions to the story of the dying thief:

> Thy presence makes my paradise,
> And where Thou art is heaven.[26]

There is, however, a waiting with Christ until the day of doom. An understanding of this may help to reconcile Catholic and Protestant beliefs, since it may be regarded as an opportunity for the soul's further education while its bliss and triumph are sure. John Goodwin has to reply to insinuations that he held that the soul as well as the body sleeps until the resurrection. He points out that the Scriptures do seem to use the metaphor of sleep to describe this period, and that in any case they are very silent concerning the soul's particular employments during it. They are only sure of its blessedness.[27]

The belief in a general Resurrection is fundamental to the Puritans as indeed to orthodox Christians of all Communions. It has been recovered by some distinguished theologians of the present century.[28] The reunion of soul and body at the Last Day, however crudely conceived by some Puritans, enshrines the truth that God judges whole personalities. The very Jewish and scriptural concept of resurrection, as distinct from immortality or survival, emphasizes the difference between eternal life bestowed by God's power and gift alone, and any native attribute of the soul, and the Christian hope is seen to be not individual salvation merely, but the resurrection of the body—of the human race.

It is significant that Thomas Brooks maintains from the Scriptures that there are degrees of glory in heaven and torments in hell. 'The more holiness you have here, the more happiness you shall have hereafter.'[29] The object of happiness will be the same for all, for it is the ever blessed God; the beatifical vision will be seen by all; all will alike be freed from all evils. Yet though the water in a hundred vessels be drawn from the same sea, the

---

[26] *MHB* (1933), No. 560; cf. No. 98, and also W. R. Inge, *Christian Mysticism*, p. 9.
[27] *Divine Authority*, p. 29.
[28] e.g. O. C. Quick, *The Gospel of the New World* (1944).
[29] *Works*, IV.368; cf. Baxter, *Works*, V.156.

amount in each depends on the individual capacity. Degrees of glory are not indeed given by merit, but by God's mercy and grace. They are answerable to different degrees of grace and holiness, labour and suffering. Brooks uses such texts as: 'Each shall receive his own reward according to his own labour'; 'One star differeth from another star in glory'; 'He that soweth sparingly shall reap also sparingly'. He appeals to the parable of the talents, the sayings about a prophet's and a righteous man's reward and the suggestion of an especial eminence for the apostles: 'Ye also shall sit upon twelve thrones judging the twelve tribes of Israel.'[30]

The joy of Heaven was often to be meditated here below. This was at once the preparation for its future blessedness and the impulse to a heavenly life upon earth. 'Let thy soule,' says Robert Bolton, 'full often soare aloft upon the wings of faith, unto the glory of the Empyrean Heaven, where God dwelleth, and bathe it selfe before hand—with many a sweet meditation in that everlasting blisse above. . . . Such fixed considerations as these, of things above, will serve as notable helps to draw and keepe thy heart Heaven-ward, and may mightily move thee to delight in God, and to hold it the sweetest life upon earth, to walke with him in the waies of Puritie and Peace.'[31] Bolton's words are a kind of anticipation of the unsurpassed soliloquies of Richard Baxter in *The Saint's Everlasting Rest*. To all the Puritans, heaven was earth perfected. 'Therefore,' says Baxter, 'put Christ no farther from you than he hath put himself, lest the divine nature be again inaccessible. Think of Christ as our own nature glorified; think of our fellow saints as men there perfected.'[32]

The excellencies are as those of this life in all its aspects, only so much more! Pleasures of sense, the delights of knowledge, the wonders of creation, all point to the infinite bliss of the world to come. The comforts of particular providences, and of the means of grace are the foretaste of Heaven.

Judge of the lion by the paw, and of the ocean of joy by that drop which thou hast tasted. . . . If the light of the star in the night be such, or the little glimmering at the break of day, what then is the light of the sun

---

[30] 1 Corinthians 3[8], 1 Corinthians 15[41], 2 Corinthians 9[6], Luke 19[12-20], Matthew 10[41], 19[28].
[31] *Directions*, p. 65.
[32] *Works*, XXIII.377.

at noontide. If some godly men that we read of, have been over-whelmed with joy till they have cried out, "Hold Lord, stay thy hand; I can bear no more!", like weak eyes that cannot endure too great a light; O what will be my joys in heaven, when as the object of my joy shall be the most glorious God, so my soul shall be made capable of seeing and enjoying him. And though the light be ten thousand times greater than the sun's, yet my eyes shall be for ever able to behold it.[33]

[33] *Works*, XXIII.398-9. It is interesting that Baxter here describes the *summum bonum* as the Vision of God. Metaphors drawn from sense perception will always be needed by some souls, and indeed if heaven is earth perfected they are by no means out of place.

But (as *Seneca* takes with me above all his Contemporaries, because he speaketh *Things* by *Words, feelingly* and *seriously,* like a man that is past jest, so) *Herbert* speaks to *God* like one that *really believeth a God,* and whose business in the world is most *with God. Heart-work* and *Heaven-work* make up his Books.

RICHARD BAXTER on GEORGE HERBERT

There were Puritans before the name was invented, and there probably will continue to be Puritans long after it has ceased to be a common epithet. Chaucer met one on the road to Canterbury. . . . The parson, says Chaucer, was a learned man devoted to teaching and caring for his people. He was poor, but 'he coude in litel thing han suffisaunce'. When sufficiently provoked, he rebuked the obstinate whether of high or low estate, but his real business was to lead men to heaven by fair words and good example. He was discreet and benign of speech, not 'daungerous ne digne'. Above all

> *This noble ensample to his sheep he yaf,*
> *That first he wroghte, and afterward he taughte :—*
> *And this figure he added eek ther-to,*
> *That if gold ruste, what shal iren do?*
> *. . . Christes lore and his apostles twelve*
> *He taughte, and first he folwed it himselve.*

WILLIAM HALLER

CHAPTER TEN

CONCLUSION

THE serious professor of religion will not be perturbed if he meets with opprobium and scorn from his fellow men. The very name 'Puritan' smacks of over-scrupulousness, and there have never been wanting those, like the neighbours of the youthful Richard Baxter, who have coupled it with 'Precisian' and 'Hypocrite' in the abuse of the sober.[1] If an eminent authority from another place is to be believed, 'the value we have given to that word (Puritan) is one of the really solid triumphs of the last hundred years. By it we rescue annually thousands of humans from temperance, chastity, and sobriety of life.'[2] But the Christian will not exaggerate the differences between himself and his fellows. If he is an Arminian, he will proclaim a divine mercy which all can share—'harlots and publicans and thieves'; if a Calvinist, the sight of sin will make him hasten to acknowledge: 'There but for the grace of God go I.'[3] The Puritans were not Pharisees. Nor did they wish to be thought eccentric. Robert Bolton's *Directions for a Comfortable Walking with God* begins with the declaration: 'The Servants of God are men of singularitie: I meane it not in respect of any fantasticalnesse of opinion, furiousnesse of zeale, or turbulencie of faction, truely so called: but in respect of abstinence from sin, puritie of heart, and holinesse of life.'[4] Richard Alleine, to whom Methodists owe their Covenant Service, begins his *Vindiciae Pietatis*, which Wesley reprints in the *Christian Library*, by seeking to rehabilitate the term 'Precisian'. 'Christians must be Precisians.' But he goes on to say that he means 'Scripture Precisians', that is 'sincere, circumspect Christians', *not* Pharisees, or Enthusiasts or 'Phreneticks'—that is, sons of violence or contention.[5]

---

[1] See *Reliquiae Baxterianae*, I.i.
[2] The Arch-fiend Screwtape in C. S. Lewis, *The Screwtape Letters* (1942), p. 55.
[3] This saying has often been attributed to Richard Baxter, but actually belongs to the Cambridge Reformer and Martyr, John Bradford.
[4] op. cit., p. 2.
[5] op. cit.; Wesley's *Christian Library*, Vol. XVIII.

If then, as we have had opportunity to confirm, the Puritan considered himself to be nothing other than a simple scriptural Christian, we shall expect that his piety will have much in common with the great devotional traditions of Christendom. In all serious Christianity there have been three elements: (1) A strictness of discipline; (2) a desire for holiness; (3) a personal devotion to Christ. We can claim to have found all three in Puritanism.

DISCIPLINE

This is what many sympathetic writers of other traditions would consider to be the whole of Puritanism.[6] That is far from the truth, but our authors take their place beside the innumerable host of those who have heard the call of Christ to self-denial, to watching and fasting and prayer, and, with His great Apostle, have sought to put on the whole armour of God.

There is a characteristic of Puritanism which it shares with post-Renaissance piety, and which has been described by Max Weber —it 'took rational Christian asceticism and its methodical habits out of the monasteries and placed them in the service of active life in the world'.[7] In our day, we have seen a revival of monasticism in England, and a reassessment of its value. No longer is the invalid notion of the 'double standard' to the fore.[8] Monasticism is interpreted in terms of 'the differences of function within the one Body'.[9] Thus it may be a corrective to the utilitarian and activist conception of the Christian life. But there is always the danger that the idea of a double standard may be implicit in the exaltation of the 'religious life' (itself a perilous term), even when the cell is not regarded as an escape, 'a safe refuge from the provoking of all men and the strife of tongues'.[10] The Puritan insistence that the full Christian life could be lived in the natural relationships of family and commerce is the more excellent way, and, as various movements from the Pilgrim Fathers to the 'Brüderhof' have shown, it need not be suspended in persecution and

---

[6] e.g. 'Some element of Puritanism is essential to all true religion', J. W. C. Wand, *Seven Steps to Heaven* (London, 1956), p. 36.

[7] *The Protestant Ethic*, p. 235, n.79.

[8] See K. E. Kirk, *The Vision of God*, e.g. pp. 242-4, 517-34.

[9] cf. G. S. Shaw and E. Hayman in *Ways of Worship*, p. 336.

[10] W. R. Inge, *Christian Mysticism*, p. 42.

war, although it was for these trials that the Puritans realized the value of celibacy.

There has always been a danger that Christian discipline would over-reach itself by imposing burdens too grievous to be borne or enforcing a dictatorship of conscience. Puritanism does not altogether escape this tendency. It may be most obvious to men of the twentieth century in sabbatarianism, in which Puritan piety comes within range of the criticism that it is dominated by the Old Testament. One could wish for a sole emphasis on Jesus and the Resurrection in Puritan teaching about the Lord's Day. Even so, it is not for us, who have our own problems of order and discipline within the Church, to be unduly censorious of the observance of that institution which the Puritans regarded as the keystone of the corporate life of believers, and of personal piety. We cannot hope to recover the Puritan Sunday, but we must seek its equivalent in devotional and educational discipline.

HOLINESS

Calvinists and Arminians charged each other (and the Roman Catholics and sectaries!) with a virtual antinomianism, but in fact, both were passionately devoted to the pursuit of holy living. This was the aim of their casuistry, and they were so convinced of it, that in the urgent effort to promote growth in grace, they adapted the moral theology of the Schoolmen. Even within that central Puritan tradition which has been our study, we can discern differences between those who regarded sainthood as entirely a matter of God's election, those who were concerned with the human response to divine grace, and those whose desire for God compelled them to seek His likeness. But, in practice, these all were dedicated to good works, not in order to earn salvation, but as the expression of that sonship which they believed was their destiny in Christ. Modern liberal Christians have spoken of religion as being co-extensive with life, and of Christ as the Lord of every realm. It may be doubted whether they have made as thorough-going an attempt to relate the Gospel to the whole of living as the Puritans, whom posterity has maligned as narrow and tyrannical.

Dr H. B. Workman once committed himself to the statement that 'Protestantism has too often driven out the eagle to save the sparrows', that is, as Pourrat suggests, it has been incapable of love and the heroic virtues, and has failed to cultivate exceptional saintliness in offering to the generality of mankind a life of moral respectability.[11] This is the kind of criticism that any movement has to meet which seeks to Christianize ordinary life, and whose failures are unimaginative *bourgeois* not libertines. But it may be doubted whether it is a fair comment either on Protestantism in general, or Puritanism in particular. The history of the Puritan tradition is not without its heroes, whether we think of the early American colonists or of David Livingstone, and if we recognize the Puritan influence upon the early Methodists and the evangelical missionaries, we need not look far for saints.

DEVOTION TO CHRIST

There have been several types of devotion to the Person of Christ throughout Christian history, and we find echoes of most of them in Puritan writings. The chronology of their development is uncertain, so we will take them in what seems to be a logical order.

(a) Devotion to the sacred humanity

This is for ever associated with the name of Bernard of Clairvaux. The Puritans honoured him and echoed his raptures, though they realized that to isolate the human life of Jesus in devotion is to do less than justice to God's vast design. The proportion of their faith was that of the Gospels themselves. They thought most of the sacred humanity in the Passion, at the point where earth and heaven meet, and history stands still. They rejoiced above all in what a modern theologian has called the human life of God. Christ can as soon cease to be God as cease to be man. God may be for ever said to be compassionate as a man.

Thus the Puritan looked beyond the bleeding wounds of Calvary to the interceding Saviour at God's right hand. His hope of mercy lay in the Sacred Heart in Heaven. The Catholic who uses the visual crucifix, needs the Virgin and the Saints to intercede for him even with the Triumphant Christ; the Puritan needed no other mediator than the Son of God Himself.

The dogma of the Ascension is as important for Puritan

[11] H. B. Workman, quoted K. E. Kirk, *The Vision of God*, p. 521; cf. P. Pourrat, *Christian Spirituality*, III.70.

spirituality as Dr Torrance has shown it to be for Calvinist eschatology.[12] Dr Nuttall has quoted from a letter of Philip Doddridge an extract which shows something of what this could mean in practice:

Away, then, my dear friend, with every mournful view. Begin, begin upon earth the songs of heaven. Tell all that are around you what God hath done for your soul, and what he is still doing. . . . Look, my dear brother, look to Jesus, our rising, ascending Lord. Behold him pointing upward amidst the raptures with which he was leaving this poor world of ours; pointing upward and saying, 'I ascend to my father and your father, to my and to your God.'[13]

(b) Mystical devotion

We have noticed some signs of a desire for an even more immediate communion with Christ than is expressed in the contemplation of His sufferings or His finished work. John Preston's great soliloquy yearns for Christ, not in any past event or even as He is in Heaven, but 'here below, in the Church and in myselfe'. Many Puritans expound the Song of Songs. But this is mysticism within the context of the historic Gospel and the Church. Our authors do not go beyond the divine election and justification.

(c) Devotion to Christ in the Sacrament

There is none of the more individualistic sacramental piety in Puritanism. The Sacraments are Church ordinances, and derive all their significance from what God in Christ has done for His people. The Passion is meditated, and the broken bread and poured-out wine are seen as tokens of a Crucified Redeemer, but there is no danger of a cult of the sacred elements, because all the power and efficacy of the rite comes from Him who reigns above, and whose final triumph it foreshadows.

Puritan devotion, then, is Christo-centric, but Christ is always seen in His relation to God and to the purpose of God. He is not confined to the Incarnation, to the altar, or to the warmed heart of believers. He is in the Old Testament as well as the New, and everywhere He is transcendent, and His sway is cosmic. This delivers Puritan devotion from sentimentality, and even from the innocent preciosity of St Francis of Sales, with his bouquets and

---

[12] *Kingdom and Church*, especially pp. 101 ff.
[13] G. F. Nuttall, *Richard Baxter, and Philip Doddridge*, p. 16.

his apricots. But there is no lack of ardour. Puritan piety is, in the language of the time, 'affectionate'. It does not seek to attain states beyond those of rational emotion, but at times all the love and desire of their whole being is poured into the soliloquies of the Puritan saints. The God and Father of Jesus Christ is the supreme reality of their souls. They lift up their hearts and their voices to Him, for they owe all their standing to His grace, and would take nothing but from His hand. If He bestow it, whether it be the bread of bodily life, the bread of the Sacrament, or the bread of tears, it must needs be good.

THE CONTRAST WITH CATHOLIC PIETY

There is one vital contrast between Catholic devotion and Protestant as represented in our Puritans. Catholicism has taken over the neo-Platonist doctrine of the 'three ways'. The Christian life has three stages—Purgation, Illumination, and Union. For the Puritan, too, it may be said that there are three ways, but these are Justification, Sanctification, Glorification. *Union with Christ is not the end but the beginning of the Christian Life.* It is not the result of a mystical technique, but of justification.

The end of Christ's Incarnation, Death and Resurrection, was to prepare and form an holy Nature and Frame for us in himself, to be communicated to us by Union and Fellowship with him; and not to enable us to produce in our selves the first Original of such an holy Nature by our own Endeavours. . . . All spiritual Life and Holiness is treasured up in the Fulness of Christ, and communicated to us by Union with him; therefore the accomplishing of Union with Christ is the first work of saving Grace in our Hearts, and Faith itself, being an holy Grace, and part of spiritual Life, cannot be in us before the beginning of it, but rather it is given to us, and wrought in the very working of the Union. And the way wherein it conduceth to the Union, cannot be by procuring a meer title to Christ as a Condition, because then it should be performed before the uniting work beginneth; but rather by being an Instrument, whereby we may actively receive and embrace Christ, who is already come into the Soul to take possession of it his own Habitation.[14]

This distinction may not be absolute. It may result from a difference of perspective in looking at the Christian life. The

[14] W. Marshal, *Gospel Mystery*, pp. 51, 69.

Catholic sees the long process of God's dealings with the soul, marked, if Catholic doctrine is to be restated at its best, by His infinite, agonizing patience. The Protestant is so overwhelmed by the miracle of saving grace that he sees the end in the beginning —'if thou convert me I shall be converted in an hour'[15]—even though he is, throughout the whole of his mortal life, foot-slogging the treacherous miles to the Celestial City. Moreover, the Catholic has the Gospel Sacraments and provided he does not regard them as an apparatus for the injection of 'grace' and does not overlay them with irrelevant accretions, they proclaim at the heart of his worship, the grand objectivity of God's love, and make real the believer's union with Christ in His Passion, and Risen and Ascended Glory. 'Union with Christ' is likely to be a fruitful and reconciling concept of modern Theology. But it is rightly interpreted neither as an ontological nor a psychological relationship but as the 'recapitulation' in the life of the Church of the sufferings and triumph of her Head.

There are respects in which Puritan devotion may be compared to its disadvantage with Catholic,. especially in its attitude to nature and art. Henri Talon quotes a stanza of Claudel:

Salut donc, ô monde nouveau à mes yeux, ô monde maintenant total!
O credo entier des choses visibles et invisibles, je vous accepte avec un
   coeur catholique.
Où que je tourne la tête
J'envisage l'immense octave de la création.

Talon then comments: 'We have only to read these lines to see the gulf which separates the Puritan, absorbed in the anguished contemplation of his sin and invisible reality, from the Catholic who embraces the whole world "as everlasting nourishment and as a fruit that we grip with our teeth".[16] By the Catholic, Talon means Paul Claudel. St John of the Cross, for instance, would not find the French poet altogether congenial. For him 'the creatures are only the crumbs that fall from God's table, and none but dogs will stay to pick them up'.[17] An attitude to nature will vary more with individual temperament than with ascetic system. Von Hügel has compared the sense of the divine transcendence in St John of the Cross to the 'infinite qualitative difference

15 H. Smith, *Works*, II.467.   16 *John Bunyan*, pp. 91-2.
17 W. R. Inge, *Christian Mysticism*, p. 225.

between God and man' of which Kierkegaard and Hurrell Froude (themselves of contrasting ecclesiastical positions) were so tremendously aware.[18] Some Puritans would be more interested in nature than others. Our generation may see in their understanding of the Cosmic Christ the outlines of a theology which 'includes men and nature in its vaster sweep'.[19] If the preachers as a whole appear to treat nature almost patronizingly as a storehouse of emblems, that is because they are as sure as the Psalmist, and far more sure than modern man, Who is nature's Lord. The Catholic may have more in common with the good pagan than has the Puritan, and may on the whole find it easier to approach God through nature, while the Puritan approaches nature through God. But the Catholic may as easily discover the things in nature which conceal God as reveal him. Nature may be for him a dark and terrifying mystery, which causes him to seek the protection offered by holy water, or the relics of the saints, or a shrine under every green tree. For the Puritan, the heavens themselves are opened, and all life and nature over-ruled, and evil spirits held in leash by the power of God, and Him who sits at God's right hand.

For the Puritan distrust of the more visual arts we have not to posit any Manichaean inhibitions, but a faithfulness to the Old Testament and an acute sensibility of sin, for which their age, like any other, gave them good warrant. They never forgot the evils of old Israel in the wilderness, when the people sat down to eat and drink and rose up to play—and they feared that drama might inflame the worst lusts of the flesh. They tended to ignore the creative power of art to transform squalor into beauty, which is a function of the Word of God. We may feel also that here, as in one or two other instances, their notion of sin was not sufficiently evangelical, and they thought of it more in terms of the accumulation of transgressions than as a state of alienation from God. But their precept was transcended by their practice, for who with Milton and Bunyan before him, can deny a Puritan contribution to dramatic art?

<hr>

[18] F. von Hügel, *Mystical Element*, II.343.

[19] A phrase of A. Nairne's, quoted C. E. Raven, *Science, Religion, and the Future* (Cambridge, 1943), p. 125.

THE CURE OF SOULS

It remains to ask how we, who in a different age are charged with the solemn privilege of leading souls in the way of Christ, or would ourselves seek closer communion with God, can learn from the Puritans. And first we must recognize that we have a task as urgent as that of the Puritans of the post-Reformation to re-think our moral theology. We can do it in the light of a biblical scholarship which they would have envied, and with a new knowledge of the history of the varied Christian traditions. There is no need for us to be obsessed with anti-Hellenism, but it is clear that the scholastic categories have at times unduly straitened the Gospel.

Secondly, in the Puritans themselves we can find examples of great pastors. A passionate caring and a deep tenderness under-lay much of the godly counsel, and the highway of Puritan devotion was one in which the wayfaring men, though fools, should not err. The ministry in our day must reconsider the place of the confession and absolution of sin, and of spiritual direction, in the Christian life. More personally, those of us who are set apart to the cure of souls must look to our own discipline, and learn anew that suffering is our *métier*, and perhaps also that 'brown bread and the Gospel is good fare'. When Christian teaching is joined with compassion, and deals with the ultimate questions of faith and practice, and offers men a clear goal for this world and the next, there is not much 'problem of com-munication'. Nor is pastoral concern the sole prerogative of the ordained. The Puritan householder was to order his house as the pastor his Church.

Finally, we must acknowledge the tremendous intensity, and high seriousness of the greatest Puritans, who wrote and spoke as though they had witnessed the first creation and had companied with Christ the whole way of his life from His Birth to His Glory. Always indeed are the Puritans humble before God. There is no suggestion that they have reduced the mysteries of the universe to a formula. Their language is never irreverently intimate—even Samuel Rutherford but occasionally descends to the banal—but that they knew Him in whom they believed, and had dwelt both in heaven and in hell, no reader can doubt. In spite of their laborious, and we may believe not unsuccessful, pursuit of clarity, they must often have brought the numinous into the lives of those who heard and read and obeyed. An incident in the ministry of one in the authentic Puritan tradition, an interpreter for his own age of the Puritan divines, and of the Catholic saints as well, illustrates what must have been both the effect and the explanation of some of the greatest seventeenth-century Puritan sermons. Once, after a singularly solemn New Year's sermon, a member of Free St George's Church, Edinburgh, went to the vestry to thank the minister, Alexander Whyte. He ended by saying: 'It went to my heart as if you had come straight from the Audience-Chamber.' And to this there came the quiet and grave reply: 'And perhaps I did.'[20]

[20] G. F. Barbour, *The Life of Alexander Whyte, 1836-1921*, p. 317.

INDEX OF PROPER NAMES

INDEX OF SUBJECTS